The War Scroll
The War of the Sons of Light
Against the Sons of Darkness
History, Symbols, Texts, and
Commentary

Joseph Lumpkin

Joseph Lumpkin

The War Scroll
The War of the Sons of Light
Against the Sons of Darkness
History, Symbols, Texts, and Commentary

For information about first time authors, contact Fifth
Estate
Blountsville, AL 35031

Cover Designed by An Quigley
Printed on acid-free paper

Library of Congress Control No: 2014919256
ISBN: 9781936533480

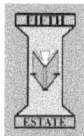

Fifth Estate, 2014

Joseph Lumpkin

TheWar Scroll

TABLE OF CONTENTS

CHAPTER ONE
INTRODUCTION

The War Scroll, popularly known as "The War of the Sons of Light Against the Sons of Darkness," is one of the seven original Dead Sea Scrolls discovered in Qumran in 1947 and holds the Qumran library designator of "1QM," meaning it was produced from the dig of cave 1. The scroll is constructed of at least twenty columns, of which only 19 remain intact or legible. The first 14–19 lines out of approximately 22 lines of the columns are preserved. Later in the Quram dig another copy or version of the scroll was found in cave 4. The 4Q491-497 fragments were published by Baillet in the 40 volume set published by Oxford Press titled, "Discoveries in the Judean Desert". It comprises a shorter version of the War Scroll. The War Scroll is a very important piece of literature in our understanding of the concepts of divine justice and retribution held by the Jewish community in their time of persecution by Rome.

The scroll reflects a belief that in the end times evil would be eradicated by the Power of God and his Sons of Light. It also indicates a belief that the times in which the scroll was written were merging with the end of days.

The scroll reflects how the Qumran community

saw itself as a righteous light in the world. They saw themselves solidly on the side of good, and as God's army, they would fight evil in the world.

The symbolism used in the scroll uses the names of 'Kittim of Asshur', which evokes Rome and allegorically stands for any evil nation or opponent of good.

Like the Book of Daniel, this text calls for the reader to persist in fighting evil and to resist Roman, or any other imperial or evil culture. Like other heroic sagas, the War Scroll is fascinated by the details of armament and is replete in the descriptions of weapons and tactics. The final battle's last engagement is the seventh strike. Seven is the number of spiritual perfection and the writers of the scroll borrow from various religious symbolisms, including scriptural numerics.

The scroll is written in Hebrew in a square Herodian script and is dated to the late first century BCE or early first century CE. Seven additional fragments (4Q491-497) with similar contents have also been found, but the relationship between these texts to 1QM is not entirely clear; they may represent an earlier version of the War Scroll, or source materials on which the War Scroll was based.

It is possible that The War of the Messiah is the conclusion to this document. The War of the Messiah is a six-line fragment, commonly referred to as the "Pierced Messiah" text. It is also written in a Herodian script of the first half of the first century C.E. and refers to a Messiah from the Branch of David, to a judgment, and to a killing. The fragment reads:

"Isaiah the prophet: The thickets of the forest will be cut down with an axe and Lebanon by a majestic one will fall. And there shall come forth a shoot from the stump of Jesse the Branch of David and they will enter into judgment with [and the Prince of the Congregation, the Branch of David] will kill him by stroke]s and by wounds. And a Priest of renown will command the slain of the Kittim"

Although the War Scroll is called "apocalyptic" by most scholars, it lacks certain elements to place it firmly in that genre. Part of the dispute in placing the War Scroll in the list of apocalyptic works arises from the difference of the use of the word in general parlance versus theological venues.

In modern English, the noun 'apocalypse' and the

related adjective 'apocalyptic' have come to connote a catastrophe of cosmic proportions" (Collins, 1997, pg.1).

The scroll certainly fits that description. However, to a theologian the word has a slightly different meaning. The word "apocalypse" means a revelation, or revealing. "Revelation" is from Anglo-French apocalipse, from Late Latin apocalypsis, from Greek apokalypsis, which means to uncover. Normally, apocalyptic texts contain a messiah, that reveals heaven to his followers. This work is not, strictly speaking, an apocalypse because it lacks a "messianic" figure, and has no heavenly revelations. It does, however, describe a great war in which God himself intervenes. If the fragments of the War of the Messiah are in fact the ending to the War Scroll, it would definitely be considered an apocalyptic text in every sense of the word.

Two time periods have been put forward and defended as the most probable time of composition of the War Scroll. The Seleucid period and the Roman period have been proposed. The Seleucid period proposals include the very beginning of the Maccabean Revolt (165 or 164 BCE), the height of Jonathan's military power (143 BCE), and the reign of John Hyrcanus (135-104 BCE). The scholars that believe that the date of composition occurred during the Roman period put forward a date from the middle of the first century BCE to the first decade of the first century CE.

The War Scroll's description of the weaponry and tactics led Yigael Yadin to assign the composition of the scroll to a date between the capture of Jerusalem by Pompey (65 BCE) and the death of Herod (4 BCE). More recently, author Russell Gmirkin, in "The War Scroll and Roman Weaponry Reconsidered," disagrees with Yadin's analysis and assigns the weaponry described in the War Scroll to the second century BCE. Lt. Col. Peter Fromm (US Army Ret.) sides with Gmirkin also assigning the army and weaponry described in the War Scroll to the second century BCE. Thus, most of the evidence points to a period between 65 BCE and 165 BCE.

Scholars have been unable to determine the exact author of the text. The unity and cohesiveness of the manuscript leads some, such as Jean Carmignac and Yigael Yadin, to believe that it was written or compiled by a single writer. Most scholars believe, at this point, that it is a composite document, copied from many source documents by one scribe.

The war between good and evil, described in the scroll can be seen clearly against the backdrop of a long biblical tradition concerning a final war at the End of Days as described in Ezekiel, Daniel, Revelation, and Enoch.

Several copies of the books of Enoch and of Daniel were found at the Qumran site, leaving no doubt that they exercised a profound influence on the Dead Sea sect. "However, their worldview is not simply adopted and reproduced in the sectarian documents. They represent a source for the ideology of the sect, not an expression of it" (Collin, 1997, pg.11).

Another significant part of the War Scroll which we will see played out in future doomsday sects, is how they saw themselves in relation with their core religion . It has been shown in research that the "final battle between good and evil" in the War Scroll, the book of Daniel, and other apocalyptic literature, such as Enoch, differs in one way that sets the tone for the Qumran community culture and view of itself. The community and the nation did not have a peaceful coexistence. The stress between the Qumran community and the Jewish people in general seemed to be of the same dynamics as any extreme fundamental community that claims to be holier, more righteous, or closer to God than other sects or religions.

"The Dead Sea sect had a stressful relationship with national, ethnic, Israel. It was patently not coterminous with the Jewish people and so could claim at most to be a remnant of Israel" (Yadin, 1962, p.59).

Still, the people at Qumran considered themselves the real Israel, the ones that God would side with in the final battle. So it seems for the first time in apocalyptic literature, the alliance system is not based solely on religion, race, or creed, but rather the actions of the individuals.

Many of the texts deal with the community and belief system, which lay out distinctions between the pious Jew, which removes himself from the temptations of the world and purifies himself under the guidelines of the community versus those of the same religion that continue to soil their souls by interaction with the world in general and the Roman influence pervading at the time.

Who wrote the War Scroll?
The Dead Sea Scrolls are usually thought to have been produced by a group known as the Essenes.

The Essenes were a group of Jews that wished to adhere as close as possible to the letter of the law as they interpreted the Torah. In protest to what they perceived as the religious shortcomings of the Pharisee and Sadducee sects they began their own fundamentalist sect by venturing out in the desert to prepare the way of the Lord, following the commands of the prophet Isaiah, as they believed them to be.

The group abandoned the worldliness of Jerusalem, the error of Temple worship, and the influence of the Romans, which they believed had tainted the Jews of their time. They had been around for a hundred years at the time the War Scroll was written. At the reign of Herod and his sons the Essene community was rising in popularity as protests were growing against Roman rule and their worldliness.

The Essenes were an apocalyptic sect of Judaism. They believed themselves to be the only group pious enough to perform the true form of their religion. They thought of themselves as righteous, the remnant, the chosen ones, and the elect. Thus, they believed themselves to be the ones who would stand with God against the evil ones of the coming age.

The basis for that understanding is their reading of Scripture, applied specifically to themselves.

The Essenes interpreted Scripture, such as Isaiah and many passages in the Torah itself, to suggest that the course of Judaism was in decline. They believed far too many people were becoming worldly and this meant the end of days and the evil of that age was moving inexorably upon them.

In their understanding, there would come a day when the Lord will revisit the Earth with power and wage war against non-believers and evil doers. After defeating the Gentiles and unclean Jews He would establish a new kingdom for Judaism. They would be in God's army and the people who would occupy the new Jerusalem. This massive war, destruction of non-believers, and establishment of a holy kingdom is part of that apocalyptic mind set.

The Essenes had a leader called "The Teacher of Righteousness, but he was not the Messiah. God himself was seen by some of these groups to be the ruler in a type of Theocracy. It has been suggested that Jesus, himself, as well as John the Baptist, were members of this group.

Essenes have been referred to as part of the "Dead Sea Community." At least most scholars believe them to be the same people. The community remained totally isolated from other Jews and from the rest of the Roman world. Their scrolls reveal that they saw themselves as the new sacred community, who were waiting for the time the Temple would be reconstituted, reconstructed and rebuilt, and the priestly group from the Essenes would take over the Temple in Jerusalem.

The Essense followed a calendar based on the moon. The believed the other Jews followed the wrong calendar, thus performing rituals at the incorrect times, officiating improperly before the Lord. All this impurity would hasten the end times.

One scenario for the last days is the scroll "War of the Sons of Light against the Sons of Darkness", also called "The War Scroll." The Essenes see themselves clearly as the Sons of Light... the Sons of Darkness are everybody else. Jews who did not follow the Essense way, gentiles, priests of other sects, all non-Essene people are together under the category of the Sons of Darkness, and will be the enemies in a major battle, ending is a cataclysmic struggle between unclean men and the cosmic forces of evil and the cosmic forces of good, God, his Angels, and the Essenes.

In this gigantic struggle, four Archangels will fight along side the Sons of Light, against the Sons of Darkness and the forces of evil. Indeed, Michael will lead the armies of the Sons of Light. This will end with a victory for the Sons of Light.

The Scroll does not clearly spell out what will happen after the victory as clearly as we might have liked. After the last major battle and the victory songs of praise, we are left simply knowing good defeated evil and all will be well.

To get a better perspective on the place of the War Scroll in end time literature, let us quickly look at what Ezekiel, Daniel, Revelation, and Enoch say about the same end times covered by the War Scroll.

Chapter Two
Comparative Texts

(Ezekiel 38–39;

Ezekiel 38 New International Version (NIV)
The Lord's Great Victory Over the Nations

1 The word of the Lord came to me: 2 "Son of man, set your face against Gog, of the land of Magog, the chief prince of [a] Meshek and Tubal; prophesy against him 3 and say: "This is what the Sovereign Lord says: I am against you, Gog, chief prince of[b] Meshek and Tubal. 4 I will turn you around, put hooks in your jaws and bring you out with your whole army — your horses, your horsemen fully armed, and a great horde with large and small shields, all of them brandishing their swords. 5 Persia, Cush[c] and Put will be with them, all with shields and helmets, 6 also Gomer with all its troops, and Beth Togarmah from the far north with all its troops — the many nations with you.
7 Get ready; be prepared, you and all the hordes gathered about you, and take command of them. 8 After many days you will be called to arms. In future years you will invade a land that has recovered from war, whose people were gathered from many nations to the mountains of Israel, which had long been desolate. They had been brought out from the nations, and now all of them

live in safety. 9 You and all your troops and the
many nations with you will go up, advancing like a
storm; you will be like a cloud covering the land."
10 This is what the Sovereign Lord says: "On that
day thoughts will come into your mind and you
will devise an evil scheme. 11 You will say, I will
invade a land of unwalled villages; I will attack a
peaceful and unsuspecting people — all of them
living without walls and without gates and bars. 12
I will plunder and loot and turn my hand against
the resettled ruins and the people gathered from
the nations, rich in livestock and goods, living at
the center of the land.[d]" 13 Sheba and Dedan and
the merchants of Tarshish and all her villages[e]
will say to you, "Have you come to plunder? Have
you gathered your hordes to loot, to carry off silver
and gold, to take away livestock and goods and to
seize much plunder?

14 Therefore, son of man, prophesy and say to Gog:
'This is what the Sovereign Lord says: In that day,
when my people Israel are living in safety, will you
not take notice of it? 15 You will come from your
place in the far north, you and many nations with
you, all of them riding on horses, a great horde, a
mighty army. 16 You will advance against my
people Israel like a cloud that covers the land. In
days to come, Gog, I will bring you against my
land, so that the nations may know me when I am

proved holy through you before their eyes."
17 This is what the Sovereign Lord says: You are the one I spoke of in former days by my servants the prophets of Israel. At that time they prophesied for years that I would bring you against them. 18 This is what will happen in that day: When Gog attacks the land of Israel, my hot anger will be aroused, declares the Sovereign Lord. 19 In my zeal and fiery wrath I declare that at that time there shall be a great earthquake in the land of Israel. 20 The fish in the sea, the birds in the sky, the beasts of the field, every creature that moves along the ground, and all the people on the face of the earth will tremble at my presence. The mountains will be overturned, the cliffs will crumble and every wall will fall to the ground. 21 I will summon a sword against Gog on all my mountains, declares the Sovereign Lord. Every man's sword will be against his brother. 22 I will execute judgment on him with plague and bloodshed; I will pour down torrents of rain, hailstones and burning sulfur on him and on his troops and on the many nations with him. 23 And so I will show my greatness and my holiness, and I will make myself known in the sight of many nations. Then they will know that I am the Lord."

Footnotes:

A Ezekiel 38:2 Or the prince of Rosh,

B Ezekiel 38:3 Or Gog, prince of Rosh,

C Ezekiel 38:5 That is, the upper Nile region

D Ezekiel 38:12 The Hebrew for this phrase means the navel of the earth.

E Ezekiel 38:13 Or her strong lions

Ezekiel 39 New International Version (NIV)

39 "Son of man, prophesy against Gog and say: 'This is what the Sovereign Lord says: I am against you, Gog, chief prince of[a] Meshek and Tubal. 2 I will turn you around and drag you along. I will bring you from the far north and send you against the mountains of Israel. 3 Then I will strike your bow from your left hand and make your arrows drop from your right hand. 4 On the mountains of Israel you will fall, you and all your troops and the nations with you. I will give you as food to all kinds of carrion birds and to the wild animals. 5 You will fall in the open field, for I have spoken, declares the Sovereign Lord. 6 I will send fire on Magog and on those who live in safety in the coastlands, and they will know that I am the Lord. 7 I will make known my holy name among my people Israel. I will no longer let my holy name be

profaned, and the nations will know that I the Lord am the Holy One in Israel.

8 It is coming! It will surely take place, declares the Sovereign Lord. This is the day I have spoken of.

9 Then those who live in the towns of Israel will go out and use the weapons for fuel and burn them up—the small and large shields, the bows and arrows, the war clubs and spears. For seven years they will use them for fuel.

10 They will not need to gather wood from the fields or cut it from the forests, because they will use the weapons for fuel. And they will plunder those who plundered them and loot those who looted them, declares the Sovereign Lord."

11 "On that day I will give Gog a burial place in Israel, in the valley of those who travel east of the Sea. It will block the way of travelers, because Gog and all his hordes will be buried there. So it will be called the Valley of Hamon Gog.[b]

12 "'For seven months the Israelites will be burying them in order to cleanse the land.

13 All the people of the land will bury them, and the day I display my glory will be a memorable day for them, declares the Sovereign Lord.

14 People will be continually employed in cleansing the land. They will spread out across the land and, along with others, they will bury any bodies that are lying on the ground."

After the seven months they will carry out a more detailed search.

15 As they go through the land, anyone who sees a human bone will leave a marker beside it until the gravediggers bury it in the Valley of Hamon Gog, 16 near a town called Hamonah.[c] And so they will cleanse the land."

17 "Son of man, this is what the Sovereign Lord says: Call out to every kind of bird and all the wild animals: 'Assemble and come together from all around to the sacrifice I am preparing for you, the great sacrifice on the mountains of Israel. There you will eat flesh and drink blood. 18 You will eat the flesh of mighty men and drink the blood of the princes of the earth as if they were rams and lambs, goats and bulls—all of them fattened animals from Bashan. 19 At the sacrifice I am preparing for you, you will eat fat till you are glutted and drink blood till you are drunk. 20 At my table you will eat your fill of horses and riders, mighty men and soldiers of every kind," declares the Sovereign Lord.

21 "I will display my glory among the nations, and all the nations will see the punishment I inflict and the hand I lay on them.

22 From that day forward the people of Israel will know that I am the Lord their God.

23 And the nations will know that the people of Israel went into exile for their sin, because they

were unfaithful to me. So I hid my face from them and handed them over to their enemies, and they all fell by the sword.

24 I dealt with them according to their uncleanness and their offenses, and I hid my face from them.

25 Therefore this is what the Sovereign Lord says: I will now restore the fortunes of Jacob[d] and will have compassion on all the people of Israel, and I will be zealous for my holy name.

26 They will forget their shame and all the unfaithfulness they showed toward me when they lived in safety in their land with no one to make them afraid.

27 When I have brought them back from the nations and have gathered them from the countries of their enemies, I will be proved holy through them in the sight of many nations.

28 Then they will know that I am the Lord their God, for though I sent them into exile among the nations, I will gather them to their own land, not leaving any behind.

29 I will no longer hide my face from them, for I will pour out my Spirit on the people of Israel," declares the Sovereign Lord.

Footnotes:

  A Ezekiel 39:1 Or Gog, prince of Rosh,

  B Ezekiel 39:11 Hamon Gog means hordes of

Gog.

   C Ezekiel 39:16 Hamonah means horde.

   D Ezekiel 39:25 Or now bring Jacob back from captivity.

Daniel 7: 1–28),

Daniel 7 New International Version (NIV)
Daniel's Dream of Four Beasts

1 In the first year of Belshazzar king of Babylon, Daniel had a dream, and visions passed through his mind as he was lying in bed. He wrote down the substance of his dream.

2 Daniel said: "In my vision at night I looked, and there before me were the four winds of heaven churning up the great sea.

3 Four great beasts, each different from the others, came up out of the sea.

4 The first was like a lion, and it had the wings of an eagle. I watched until its wings were torn off and it was lifted from the ground so that it stood on two feet like a human being, and the mind of a human was given to it.

5 And there before me was a second beast, which looked like a bear. It was raised up on one of its sides, and it had three ribs in its mouth between its

teeth. It was told, 'Get up and eat your fill of flesh!
6 After that, I looked, and there before me was
another beast, one that looked like a leopard. And
on its back it had four wings like those of a bird.
This beast had four heads, and it was given
authority to rule.
7 After that, in my vision at night I looked, and
there before me was a fourth beast — terrifying and
frightening and very powerful. It had large iron
teeth; it crushed and devoured its victims and
trampled underfoot whatever was left. It was
different from all the former beasts, and it had ten
horns.
8 While I was thinking about the horns, there
before me was another horn, a little one, which
came up among them; and three of the first horns
were uprooted before it. This horn had eyes like the
eyes of a human being and a mouth that spoke
boastfully.
9 As I looked,
thrones were set in place,
    and the Ancient of Days took his seat.
His clothing was as white as snow;
    the hair of his head was white like wool.
His throne was flaming with fire,
    and its wheels were all ablaze.
10 A river of fire was flowing,
    coming out from before him.

Thousands upon thousands attended him;
   ten thousand times ten thousand stood before
him. The court was seated, and the books were
opened.
11 Then I continued to watch because of the
boastful words the horn was speaking. I kept
looking until the beast was slain and its body
destroyed and thrown into the blazing fire.
12 (The other beasts had been stripped of their
authority, but were allowed to live for a period of
time.)

Daniel's Dream

13 In my vision at night I looked, and there before
me was one like a son of man,[a] coming with the
clouds of heaven. He approached the Ancient of
Days and was led into his presence.
14 He was given authority, glory and sovereign
power; all nations and peoples of every language
worshiped him. His dominion is an everlasting
dominion that will not pass away, and his kingdom
is one that will never be destroyed.

The Interpretation of the Dream

15 I, Daniel, was troubled in spirit, and the visions
that passed through my mind disturbed me.

16 I approached one of those standing there and asked him the meaning of all this.

So he told me and gave me the interpretation of these things:

17 The four great beasts are four kings that will rise from the earth.

18 But the holy people of the Most High will receive the kingdom and will possess it forever — yes, for ever and ever.

19 Then I wanted to know the meaning of the fourth beast, which was different from all the others and most terrifying, with its iron teeth and bronze claws — the beast that crushed and devoured its victims and trampled underfoot whatever was left.

20 I also wanted to know about the ten horns on its head and about the other horn that came up, before which three of them fell — the horn that looked more imposing than the others and that had eyes and a mouth that spoke boastfully.

21 As I watched, this horn was waging war against the holy people and defeating them,

22 until the Ancient of Days came and pronounced judgment in favor of the holy people of the Most High, and the time came when they possessed the kingdom.

23 He gave me this explanation: 'The fourth beast is

a fourth kingdom that will appear on earth. It will be different from all the other kingdoms and will devour the whole earth, trampling it down and crushing it.

24 The ten horns are ten kings who will come from this kingdom. After them another king will arise, different from the earlier ones; he will subdue three kings.

25 He will speak against the Most High and oppress his holy people and try to change the set times and the laws. The holy people will be delivered into his hands for a time, times and half a time.[b]

26 But the court will sit, and his power will be taken away and completely destroyed forever.

27 Then the sovereignty, power and greatness of all the kingdoms under heaven will be handed over to the holy people of the Most High. His kingdom will be an everlasting kingdom, and all rulers will worship and obey him.

28 This is the end of the matter. I, Daniel, was deeply troubled by my thoughts, and my face turned pale, but I kept the matter to myself."

Footnotes:

A Daniel 7:13 The Aramaic phrase bar enash means human being. The phrase son of man is retained here because of its use in the New

Testament as a title of Jesus, probably based largely on this verse.

B Daniel 7:25 Or for a year, two years and half a year

Daniel 8 New International Version (NIV)
Daniel's Vision of a Ram and a Goat

1 In the third year of King Belshazzar's reign, I, Daniel, had a vision, after the one that had already appeared to me.
2 In my vision I saw myself in the citadel of Susa in the province of Elam; in the vision I was beside the Ulai Canal.
3 I looked up, and there before me was a ram with two horns, standing beside the canal, and the horns were long. One of the horns was longer than the other but grew up later.
4 I watched the ram as it charged toward the west and the north and the south. No animal could stand against it, and none could rescue from its power. It did as it pleased and became great.
5 As I was thinking about this, suddenly a goat with a prominent horn between its eyes came from the west, crossing the whole earth without touching the ground.
6 It came toward the two-horned ram I had seen

standing beside the canal and charged at it in great
rage.

7 I saw it attack the ram furiously, striking the ram
and shattering its two horns. The ram was
powerless to stand against it; the goat knocked it to
the ground and trampled on it, and none could
rescue the ram from its power.

8 The goat became very great, but at the height of
its power the large horn was broken off, and in its
place four prominent horns grew up toward the
four winds of heaven.

9 Out of one of them came another horn, which
started small but grew in power to the south and to
the east and toward the Beautiful Land.

10 It grew until it reached the host of the heavens,
and it threw some of the starry host down to the
earth and trampled on them.

11 It set itself up to be as great as the commander of
the army of the Lord; it took away the daily
sacrifice from the Lord, and his sanctuary was
thrown down.

12 Because of rebellion, the Lord's people[a] and
the daily sacrifice were given over to it. It
prospered in everything it did, and truth was
thrown to the ground.

13 Then I heard a holy one speaking, and another
holy one said to him, "How long will it take for the
vision to be fulfilled — the vision concerning the

daily sacrifice, the rebellion that causes desolation, the surrender of the sanctuary and the trampling underfoot of the Lord's people?"
14 He said to me, "It will take 2,300 evenings and mornings; then the sanctuary will be reconsecrated."

The Interpretation of the Vision

15 While I, Daniel, was watching the vision and trying to understand it, there before me stood one who looked like a man. 16 And I heard a man's voice from the Ulai calling, "Gabriel, tell this man the meaning of the vision.
17 As he came near the place where I was standing, I was terrified and fell prostrate. "Son of man,"[b] he said to me, "understand that the vision concerns the time of the end.
18 While he was speaking to me, I was in a deep sleep, with my face to the ground. Then he touched me and raised me to my feet.
19 He said: "I am going to tell you what will happen later in the time of wrath, because the vision concerns the appointed time of the end.[c]
20 The two-horned ram that you saw represents the kings of Media and Persia.
21 The shaggy goat is the king of Greece, and the large horn between its eyes is the first king.

22 The four horns that replaced the one that was broken off represent four kingdoms that will emerge from his nation but will not have the same power.

23 In the latter part of their reign, when rebels have become completely wicked, a fierce-looking king, a master of intrigue, will arise.

24 He will become very strong, but not by his own power. He will cause astounding devastation and will succeed in whatever he does. He will destroy those who are mighty, the holy people.

25 He will cause deceit to prosper, and he will consider himself superior. When they feel secure, he will destroy many and take his stand against the Prince of princes. Yet he will be destroyed, but not by human power.

26 The vision of the evenings and mornings that has been given you is true, but seal up the vision, for it concerns the distant future.

27 I, Daniel, was worn out. I lay exhausted for several days. Then I got up and went about the king's business. I was appalled by the vision; it was beyond understanding.

Footnotes:

A Daniel 8:12 Or rebellion, the armies

 B   Daniel 8:17 The Hebrew phrase ben adam means human being. The phrase son of man is retained as a form of address here because of its possible association with "Son of Man" in the New Testament.

 C   Daniel 8:19 Or because the end will be at the appointed time

Daniel 9 New International Version (NIV)
Daniel's Prayer

1 In the first year of Darius son of Xerxes[a] (a Mede by descent), who was made ruler over the Babylonian[b] kingdom—
2 in the first year of his reign, I, Daniel, understood from the Scriptures, according to the word of the Lord given to Jeremiah the prophet, that the desolation of Jerusalem would last seventy years.
3 So I turned to the Lord God and pleaded with him in prayer and petition, in fasting, and in sackcloth and ashes.
4 I prayed to the Lord my God and confessed: "Lord, the great and awesome God, who keeps his covenant of love with those who love him and keep his commandments,
5 we have sinned and done wrong. We have been wicked and have rebelled; we have turned away from your commands and laws.

6 We have not listened to your servants the prophets, who spoke in your name to our kings, our princes and our ancestors, and to all the people of the land.

7 Lord, you are righteous, but this day we are covered with shame — the people of Judah and the inhabitants of Jerusalem and all Israel, both near and far, in all the countries where you have scattered us because of our unfaithfulness to you.

8 We and our kings, our princes and our ancestors are covered with shame, Lord, because we have sinned against you.

9 The Lord our God is merciful and forgiving, even though we have rebelled against him;

10 we have not obeyed the Lord our God or kept the laws he gave us through his servants the prophets.

11 All Israel has transgressed your law and turned away, refusing to obey you. Therefore the curses and sworn judgments written in the Law of Moses, the servant of God, have been poured out on us, because we have sinned against you.

12 You have fulfilled the words spoken against us and against our rulers by bringing on us great disaster. Under the whole heaven nothing has ever been done like what has been done to Jerusalem.

13 Just as it is written in the Law of Moses, all this disaster has come on us, yet we have not sought the

favor of the Lord our God by turning from our sins and giving attention to your truth.

14 The Lord did not hesitate to bring the disaster on us, for the Lord our God is righteous in everything he does; yet we have not obeyed him.

15 Now, Lord our God, who brought your people out of Egypt with a mighty hand and who made for yourself a name that endures to this day, we have sinned, we have done wrong.

16 Lord, in keeping with all your righteous acts, turn away your anger and your wrath from Jerusalem, your city, your holy hill. Our sins and the iniquities of our ancestors have made Jerusalem and your people an object of scorn to all those around us.

17 Now, our God, hear the prayers and petitions of your servant. For your sake, Lord, look with favor on your desolate sanctuary.

18 Give ear, our God, and hear; open your eyes and see the desolation of the city that bears your Name. We do not make requests of you because we are righteous, but because of your great mercy.

19 Lord, listen! Lord, forgive! Lord, hear and act! For your sake, my God, do not delay, because your city and your people bear your Name.

The Seventy "Sevens

20 While I was speaking and praying, confessing

my sin and the sin of my people Israel and making
my request to the Lord my God for his holy hill —
21 while I was still in prayer, Gabriel, the man I had
seen in the earlier vision, came to me in swift flight
about the time of the evening sacrifice.

22 He instructed me and said to me, "Daniel, I
have now come to give you insight and
understanding.

23 As soon as you began to pray, a word went out,
which I have come to tell you, for you are highly
esteemed. Therefore, consider the word and
understand the vision:

24 Seventy 'sevens'[c] are decreed for your people
and your holy city to finish[d] transgression, to put
an end to sin, to atone for wickedness, to bring in
everlasting righteousness, to seal up vision and
prophecy and to anoint the Most Holy Place.[e]
25 Know and understand this: From the time the
word goes out to restore and rebuild Jerusalem
until the Anointed One,[f] the ruler, comes, there
will be seven 'sevens,' and sixty-two 'sevens.' It
will be rebuilt with streets and a trench, but in
times of trouble. 26 After the sixty-two 'sevens,' the
Anointed One will be put to death and will have
nothing.[g] The people of the ruler who will come
will destroy the city and the sanctuary. The end
will come like a flood: War will continue until the
end, and desolations have been decreed. 27 He will

confirm a covenant with many for one 'seven.'[h]
In the middle of the 'seven'[i] he will put an end to
sacrifice and offering. And at the temple[j] he will
set up an abomination that causes desolation, until
the end that is decreed is poured out on him."[k][l]

Footnotes:

A Daniel 9:1 Hebrew Ahasuerus

B Daniel 9:1 Or Chaldean

C Daniel 9:24 Or 'weeks'; also in verses 25 and 26

D Daniel 9:24 Or restrain

E Daniel 9:24 Or the most holy One

F Daniel 9:25 Or an anointed one; also in verse 26

G Daniel 9:26 Or death and will have no one; or
death, but not for himself

H Daniel 9:27 Or 'week'

I Daniel 9:27 Or 'week'

J Daniel 9:27 Septuagint and Theodotion;
Hebrew wing

K Daniel 9:27 Or it

L Daniel 9:27 Or And one who causes desolation
will come upon the wing of the abominable temple,
until the end that is decreed is poured out on the
desolated city

Daniel 10 New International Version (NIV)
Daniel's Vision of a Man

1 In the third year of Cyrus king of Persia, a revelation was given to Daniel (who was called Belteshazzar). Its message was true and it concerned a great war.[a] The understanding of the message came to him in a vision.

2 At that time I, Daniel, mourned for three weeks.

3 I ate no choice food; no meat or wine touched my lips; and I used no lotions at all until the three weeks were over.

4 On the twenty-fourth day of the first month, as I was standing on the bank of the great river, the Tigris,

5 I looked up and there before me was a man dressed in linen, with a belt of fine gold from Uphaz around his waist.

6 His body was like topaz, his face like lightning, his eyes like flaming torches, his arms and legs like the gleam of burnished bronze, and his voice like the sound of a multitude.

7 I, Daniel, was the only one who saw the vision; those who were with me did not see it, but such terror overwhelmed them that they fled and hid themselves.

8 So I was left alone, gazing at this great vision; I had no strength left, my face turned deathly pale and I was helpless.

9 Then I heard him speaking, and as I listened to him, I fell into a deep sleep, my face to the ground.

10 A hand touched me and set me trembling on my hands and knees.

11 He said, "Daniel, you who are highly esteemed, consider carefully the words I am about to speak to you, and stand up, for I have now been sent to you." And when he said this to me, I stood up trembling.

12 Then he continued, "Do not be afraid, Daniel. Since the first day that you set your mind to gain understanding and to humble yourself before your God, your words were heard, and I have come in response to them.

13 But the prince of the Persian kingdom resisted me twenty-one days. Then Michael, one of the chief princes, came to help me, because I was detained there with the king of Persia.

14 Now I have come to explain to you what will happen to your people in the future, for the vision concerns a time yet to come.

15 While he was saying this to me, I bowed with my face toward the ground and was speechless.

16 Then one who looked like a man[b] touched my lips, and I opened my mouth and began to speak. I said to the one standing before me, "I am overcome with anguish because of the vision, my lord, and I feel very weak.

17 How can I, your servant, talk with you, my lord? My strength is gone and I can hardly breathe."

18 Again the one who looked like a man touched me and gave me strength.

19 "Do not be afraid, you who are highly esteemed," he said. "Peace! Be strong now; be strong."

When he spoke to me, I was strengthened and said, "Speak, my lord, since you have given me strength."

20 So he said, "Do you know why I have come to you? Soon I will return to fight against the prince of Persia, and when I go, the prince of Greece will come;

21 but first I will tell you what is written in the Book of Truth. (No one supports me against them except Michael, your prince."

Footnotes:

A Daniel 10:1 Or true and burdensome

B Daniel 10:16 Most manuscripts of the Masoretic Text; one manuscript of the Masoretic Text, Dead Sea Scrolls and Septuagint Then something that looked like a human hand

Daniel 11 New International Version (NIV)

1 And in the first year of Darius the Mede, I took my stand to support and protect him.)

The Kings of the South and the North

2 Now then, I tell you the truth: Three more kings will arise in Persia, and then a fourth, who will be far richer than all the others. When he has gained power by his wealth, he will stir up everyone against the kingdom of Greece. 3 Then a mighty king will arise, who will rule with great power and do as he pleases.

4 After he has arisen, his empire will be broken up and parceled out toward the four winds of heaven. It will not go to his descendants, nor will it have the power he exercised, because his empire will be uprooted and given to others.

5 The king of the South will become strong, but one of his commanders will become even stronger than he and will rule his own kingdom with great power.

6 After some years, they will become allies. The daughter of the king of the South will go to the king of the North to make an alliance, but she will not retain her power, and he and his power[a] will not last. In those days she will be betrayed, together with her royal escort and her father[b] and the one who supported her.

7 One from her family line will arise to take her place. He will attack the forces of the king of the North and enter his fortress; he will fight against

them and be victorious.

8 He will also seize their gods, their metal images and their valuable articles of silver and gold and carry them off to Egypt. For some years he will leave the king of the North alone.

9 Then the king of the North will invade the realm of the king of the South but will retreat to his own country.

10 His sons will prepare for war and assemble a great army, which will sweep on like an irresistible flood and carry the battle as far as his fortress.

11 Then the king of the South will march out in a rage and fight against the king of the North, who will raise a large army, but it will be defeated.

12 When the army is carried off, the king of the South will be filled with pride and will slaughter many thousands, yet he will not remain triumphant.

13 For the king of the North will muster another army, larger than the first; and after several years, he will advance with a huge army fully equipped.

14 In those times many will rise against the king of the South. Those who are violent among your own people will rebel in fulfillment of the vision, but without success. 15 Then the king of the North will come and build up siege ramps and will capture a fortified city. The forces of the South will be powerless to resist; even their best troops will not

have the strength to stand.

16 The invader will do as he pleases; no one will be able to stand against him. He will establish himself in the Beautiful Land and will have the power to destroy it.

17 He will determine to come with the might of his entire kingdom and will make an alliance with the king of the South. And he will give him a daughter in marriage in order to overthrow the kingdom, but his plans[c] will not succeed or help him.

18 Then he will turn his attention to the coastlands and will take many of them, but a commander will put an end to his insolence and will turn his insolence back on him.

19 After this, he will turn back toward the fortresses of his own country but will stumble and fall, to be seen no more.

20 His successor will send out a tax collector to maintain the royal splendor. In a few years, however, he will be destroyed, yet not in anger or in battle.

21 He will be succeeded by a contemptible person who has not been given the honor of royalty. He will invade the kingdom when its people feel secure, and he will seize it through intrigue.

22 Then an overwhelming army will be swept away before him; both it and a prince of the covenant will be destroyed.

23 After coming to an agreement with him, he will act deceitfully, and with only a few people he will rise to power.

24 When the richest provinces feel secure, he will invade them and will achieve what neither his fathers nor his forefathers did. He will distribute plunder, loot and wealth among his followers. He will plot the overthrow of fortresses — but only for a time.

25 With a large army he will stir up his strength and courage against the king of the South. The king of the South will wage war with a large and very powerful army, but he will not be able to stand because of the plots devised against him.

26 Those who eat from the king's provisions will try to destroy him; his army will be swept away, and many will fall in battle.

27 The two kings, with their hearts bent on evil, will sit at the same table and lie to each other, but to no avail, because an end will still come at the appointed time.

28 The king of the North will return to his own country with great wealth, but his heart will be set against the holy covenant. He will take action against it and then return to his own country.

29 At the appointed time he will invade the South again, but this time the outcome will be different

from what it was before.

30 Ships of the western coastlands will oppose him, and he will lose heart. Then he will turn back and vent his fury against the holy covenant. He will return and show favor to those who forsake the holy covenant.

31 His armed forces will rise up to desecrate the temple fortress and will abolish the daily sacrifice. Then they will set up the abomination that causes desolation.

32 With flattery he will corrupt those who have violated the covenant, but the people who know their God will firmly resist him.

33 Those who are wise will instruct many, though for a time they will fall by the sword or be burned or captured or plundered.

34 When they fall, they will receive a little help, and many who are not sincere will join them.

35 Some of the wise will stumble, so that they may be refined, purified and made spotless until the time of the end, for it will still come at the appointed time.

The King Who Exalts Himself

36 The king will do as he pleases. He will exalt and magnify himself above every god and will say unheard-of things against the God of gods. He will be successful until the time of wrath is completed, for what has been determined must take place.

37 He will show no regard for the gods of his ancestors or for the one desired by women, nor will he regard any god, but will exalt himself above them all.

38 Instead of them, he will honor a god of fortresses; a god unknown to his ancestors he will honor with gold and silver, with precious stones and costly gifts.

39 He will attack the mightiest fortresses with the help of a foreign god and will greatly honor those who acknowledge him. He will make them rulers over many people and will distribute the land at a price.[d]

40 At the time of the end the king of the South will engage him in battle, and the king of the North will storm out against him with chariots and cavalry and a great fleet of ships. He will invade many countries and sweep through them like a flood.

41 He will also invade the Beautiful Land. Many countries will fall, but Edom, Moab and the leaders of Ammon will be delivered from his hand.

42 He will extend his power over many countries; Egypt will not escape.

43 He will gain control of the treasures of gold and silver and all the riches of Egypt, with the Libyans and Cushites[e] in submission.

44 But reports from the east and the north will alarm him, and he will set out in a great rage to

destroy and annihilate many.

45 He will pitch his royal tents between the seas at[f] the beautiful holy mountain. Yet he will come to his end, and no one will help him.

Footnotes:

A Daniel 11:6 Or offspring

B Daniel 11:6 Or child (see Vulgate and Syriac)

C Daniel 11:17 Or but she

D Daniel 11:39 Or land for a reward

E Daniel 11:43 That is, people from the upper Nile region

F Daniel 11:45 Or the sea and

Daniel 12 New International Version (NIV)
The End Times

1 At that time Michael, the great prince who protects your people, will arise. There will be a time of distress such as has not happened from the beginning of nations until then. But at that time your people—everyone whose name is found written in the book—will be delivered.

2 Multitudes who sleep in the dust of the earth will awake: some to everlasting life, others to shame and everlasting contempt.

3 Those who are wise[a] will shine like the brightness of the heavens, and those who lead many to righteousness, like the stars for ever and

ever.

4 But you, Daniel, roll up and seal the words of the scroll until the time of the end. Many will go here and there to increase knowledge."

5 Then I, Daniel, looked, and there before me stood two others, one on this bank of the river and one on the opposite bank.

6 One of them said to the man clothed in linen, who was above the waters of the river, "How long will it be before these astonishing things are fulfilled?"

7 The man clothed in linen, who was above the waters of the river, lifted his right hand and his left hand toward heaven, and I heard him swear by him who lives forever, saying, "It will be for a time, times and half a time.[b] When the power of the holy people has been finally broken, all these things will be completed."

8 I heard, but I did not understand. So I asked, "My lord, what will the outcome of all this be?"

9 He replied, "Go your way, Daniel, because the words are rolled up and sealed until the time of the end.

10 Many will be purified, made spotless and refined, but the wicked will continue to be wicked. None of the wicked will understand, but those who are wise will understand.

11 From the time that the daily sacrifice is abolished and the abomination that causes

desolation is set up, there will be 1,290 days.
12 Blessed is the one who waits for and reaches the
end of the 1,335 days.
13 As for you, go your way till the end. You will
rest, and then at the end of the days you will rise to
receive your allotted inheritance."

Footnotes:
   A   Daniel 12:3 Or who impart wisdom
   B   Daniel 12:7 Or a year, two years and half a year

When we think of great wars we think of the battle
of Armageddon, but that is not the last battle, nor
the greatest. Therefore, let us take a look at what is
said about Armageddon and then the last battle. It
is the final battle, summed up in Revelation 19,
which has the Messiah intervening to destroy the
army of evil with the word from his mouth. This
will be summed up in Revelation 16 and Revelation
19.

Revelation 16
New International Version

The Seven Bowls of God's Wrath

1 Then I heard a loud voice from the temple saying
to the seven angels, "Go, pour out the seven bowls

of God's wrath on the earth."

2 The first angel went and poured out his bowl on the land, and ugly, festering sores broke out on the people who had the mark of the beast and worshiped its image.

3 The second angel poured out his bowl on the sea, and it turned into blood like that of a dead person, and every living thing in the sea died.

4 The third angel poured out his bowl on the rivers and springs of water, and they became blood.

5 Then I heard the angel in charge of the waters say: "You are just in these judgments, O Holy One, you who are and who were;

6 for they have shed the blood of your holy people and your prophets, and you have given them blood to drink as they deserve."

7And I heard the altar respond:

"Yes, Lord God Almighty, true and just are your judgments."

8 The fourth angel poured out his bowl on the sun, and the sun was allowed to scorch people with fire. 9 They were seared by the intense heat and they cursed the name of God, who had control over these plagues, but they refused to repent and glorify him.

10 The fifth angel poured out his bowl on the throne of the beast, and its kingdom was plunged

into darkness. People gnawed their tongues in agony

11 and cursed the God of heaven because of their pains and their sores, but they refused to repent of what they had done.

12 The sixth angel poured out his bowl on the great river Euphrates, and its water was dried up to prepare the way for the kings from the East.

13 Then I saw three impure spirits that looked like frogs; they came out of the mouth of the dragon, out of the mouth of the beast and out of the mouth of the false prophet.

14 They are demonic spirits that perform signs, and they go out to the kings of the whole world, to gather them for the battle on the great day of God Almighty.

15 "Look, I come like a thief! Blessed is the one who stays awake and remains clothed, so as not to go naked and be shamefully exposed."

16 Then they gathered the kings together to the place that in Hebrew is called Armageddon.

17 The seventh angel poured out his bowl into the air, and out of the temple came a loud voice from the throne, saying, "It is done!"

18 Then there came flashes of lightning, rumblings, peals of thunder and a severe earthquake. No earthquake like it has ever occurred since mankind has been on earth, so tremendous was the quake.

19 The great city split into three parts, and the cities of the nations collapsed. God remembered Babylon the Great and gave her the cup filled with the wine of the fury of his wrath.

20 Every island fled away and the mountains could not be found.

21 From the sky huge hailstones, each weighing about a hundred pounds,[a] fell on people. And they cursed God on account of the plague of hail, because the plague was so terrible.

Footnotes:

[a] 21 Or about 45 kilograms

Revelation 19 New International Version (NIV)
Threefold Hallelujah Over Babylon's Fall

1 After this I heard what sounded like the roar of a great multitude in heaven shouting:
"Hallelujah!
Salvation and glory and power belong to our God,
2   for true and just are his judgments.
He has condemned the great prostitute
    who corrupted the earth by her adulteries.
He has avenged on her the blood of his servants."

3 And again they shouted:
"Hallelujah!

The smoke from her goes up for ever and ever."
4 The twenty-four elders and the four living creatures fell down and worshiped God, who was seated on the throne. And they cried:
"Amen, Hallelujah!"
5 Then a voice came from the throne, saying:
"Praise our God,

all you his servants,
you who fear him,

both great and small!"
6 Then I heard what sounded like a great multitude, like the roar of rushing waters and like loud peals of thunder, shouting:
"Hallelujah!

For our Lord God Almighty reigns.
7 Let us rejoice and be glad

and give him glory!
For the wedding of the Lamb has come,

and his bride has made herself ready.
8 Fine linen, bright and clean,

was given her to wear."

(Fine linen stands for the righteous acts of God's holy people.)

9 Then the angel said to me, "Write this: Blessed are those who are invited to the wedding supper of the Lamb!" And he added, "These are the true

words of God."

10 At this I fell at his feet to worship him. But he said to me, "Don't do that! I am a fellow servant with you and with your brothers and sisters who hold to the testimony of Jesus. Worship God! For it is the Spirit of prophecy who bears testimony to Jesus."

The Heavenly Warrior Defeats the Beast

11 I saw heaven standing open and there before me was a white horse, whose rider is called Faithful and True. With justice he judges and wages war. 12 His eyes are like blazing fire, and on his head are many crowns. He has a name written on him that no one knows but he himself.

13 He is dressed in a robe dipped in blood, and his name is the Word of God.

14 The armies of heaven were following him, riding on white horses and dressed in fine linen, white and clean.

15 Coming out of his mouth is a sharp sword with which to strike down the nations. "He will rule them with an iron scepter."[a] He treads the winepress of the fury of the wrath of God Almighty.

16 On his robe and on his thigh he has this name written:

king of kings and lord of lords.

17 And I saw an angel standing in the sun, who cried in a loud voice to all the birds flying in midair, "Come, gather together for the great supper of God,

18 so that you may eat the flesh of kings, generals, and the mighty, of horses and their riders, and the flesh of all people, free and slave, great and small."

19 Then I saw the beast and the kings of the earth and their armies gathered together to wage war against the rider on the horse and his army.

20 But the beast was captured, and with it the false prophet who had performed the signs on its behalf. With these signs he had deluded those who had received the mark of the beast and worshiped its image. The two of them were thrown alive into the fiery lake of burning sulfur.

21 The rest were killed with the sword coming out of the mouth of the rider on the horse, and all the birds gorged themselves on their flesh.

Footnotes:

Revelation 19:15 Psalm 2:9

Enoch

(by Joseph Lumpkin. Published by Fifth Estate)
We will be quoting from the First Book of Enoch, or

1 Enoch, Chapters 91-93. Note from editor: at this point, the time frame and text flow becomes non sequitur. It appears the codex was not kept in sequence here. Thus, the translated pages are out of sequence. The flow of time and occurrences seems to follow the pattern listed:

91:6 to 92.1 through 92:5 then jumps to 93:1. The flow then continues from 93:1 to 93:10 and then jumps to 91:7. From 91:7 the text continues to 91:19. It then picks up again at 93:11 and continues.

If one were to attempt to put this section into a time line, the interval would link together in some fashion resembling the following:

Ten Weeks of Judgment

WEEK 1 Judgment & righteousness 93.3 Enoch's time Antediluvian (Ice-age - 16,000 B.C.)		
WEEK 2 Judgment & cleansing 93.4 Noah's time and the great flood The first judgment of the world (16,000 – 10,000 B.C)		
WEEK 3 Righteousness is planted 93.5 Abraham's time (10,000 – 2000 B.C.)		

WEEK 4 Law for all generations 93.6 Moses' time	
WEEK 4 2000 – 1400 B.C.	
WEEK 5 House of Glory 93.7 Solomon's time 1400 – 900 B.C.	
WEEK 6 Jesus ascends, temple burned, elect scattered 93.8 Jesus' time 900 B.C – 100 A.D.	
WEEK 7 Apostate generation Judgment of Fire 93.9 - 91.11 Our time The second judgment of earth. 100 A.D. - ?	
WEEK 8 A sword 91.12–13 New house, new heaven & earth Future time	
WEEK 9 The righteous judgment revealed 91.14 The judgment time	
WEEK 10 God's power is forever 91.15-16 Eternal time	

When reading the text from this point to the end of chapter 93 one should keep this flow in mind.]

[Chapter 91]
   The *Book of Warnings and Blessings of Enoch* (Chapters 91-104):

1 And now, my son Methuselah, call to me all your brothers and gather together to me all the

sons of your mother; for the word calls me, and the spirit is poured out on me, that I may show you everything that shall befall you for ever.'

2 And thereon Methuselah went and summoned to him all his brothers and assembled his relatives.

3 And he spoke to all the children of righteousness and said: 'Hear, you sons of Enoch, all the words of your father, and hearken, as you should, to the voice of my mouth; for I exhort you and say to you, beloved:

4 Love righteousness and walk in it, and draw near to righteousness without a double heart, and do not associate with those of a double heart, but walk in righteousness, my sons. And it shall guide you on good paths. And righteousness shall be your companion.'

JAM 1:6 But let him ask in faith, nothing wavering. For he that wavereth is like a wave of the sea driven with the wind and tossed. 7 For let not that man think that he shall receive any thing of the Lord. 8 A double minded man is unstable in all his ways.

5 'For I know that violence must increase on the

earth, and a great punishment will be executed on the earth, it shall be cut off from its roots, and its whole construct will be destroyed.

6 And unrighteousness shall again be complete on the earth, and all the deeds of unrighteousness and of violence and sin shall prevail a second time.

7 And when sin and unrighteousness and blasphemy and violence in all kinds of deeds increase, and apostasy and transgression and uncleanness increase; a great chastisement shall come from heaven on all these, and the holy Lord will come out with wrath and chastisement to execute judgment on earth.

2TH 2:3 Let no man deceive you by any means: for that day shall not come, except there come a falling away first, and that man of sin be revealed, the son of perdition.

8 In those days violence shall be cut off from its roots, and the roots of unrighteousness together with deceit, and they shall be destroyed from under heaven.

9 And all the idols of the heathen shall be

abandoned. And the temples burned with fire, and they shall remove them from the whole earth; and the heathen shall be cast into the judgment of fire, and shall perish in wrath and in grievous judgment for ever.

10 And the righteous shall arise from their sleep, and wisdom shall arise and be given to them.

11 And after that the roots of unrighteousness and those who plan violence and those who commit blasphemy shall be cut off, and the sinners shall be destroyed by the sword.

12 And after this there will be another week; the eighth, that of righteousness, and a sword will be given to it so that the Righteous Judgment may be executed on those who do wrong, and the sinners will be handed over into the hands of the righteous.

13 And, at its end, they will acquire Houses because of their righteousness, and a House will be built for the Great King in Glory, forever.

14 And after this, in the ninth week, the Righteous Judgment will be revealed to the whole world. And all the deeds of the impious will vanish from the whole Earth. And the world

will be written down for destruction and all men will look to the Path of Uprightness.

15 And, after this, in the tenth week, in the seventh part, there will be an Eternal Judgment that will be executed on the Watchers and the Great Eternal Heaven that will spring from the midst of the Angels.

16 And the First Heaven will vanish and pass away and a New Heaven will appear, and all the Powers of Heaven will shine forever, with light seven times as bright.

17 And after this, there will be many weeks without number, forever, in goodness and in righteousness. And from then on sin will never again be mentioned.

18 And now I tell you, my sons, and show you, the paths of righteousness and the paths of violence. I will show them to you again that you may know what will come to pass.

19 And now, hearken to me, my sons, and walk in the paths of righteousness, and walk not in the paths of violence; for all who walk in the paths of unrighteousness shall perish for ever.'

[Chapter 92]

1 The book written by Enoch {Enoch indeed wrote this complete doctrine of wisdom, (which is) praised of all men and a judge of all the earth} for all my children who shall live on the earth. And for the future generations who shall observe righteousness and peace.

2 Let not your spirit be troubled on account of the times; for the Holy and Great One has appointed days for all things.

3 And the righteous one shall arise from sleep, [Shall arise] and walk in the paths of righteousness, and all his path and conversation shall be in eternal goodness and grace.

4 He will be gracious to the righteous and give him eternal righteousness, and He will give him power so that he shall be (endowed) with goodness and righteousness. And he shall walk in eternal light.

5 And sin shall perish in darkness for ever, and shall no more be seen from that day for evermore.

[Chapter 93]

(Author's Note: Chapters 91 – 93 recount and expand on the events listed in the following weeks of prophecy. The explanation of the event are scattered in chapters 91 – 93, however, the list of events are stated clearly in the following list of weeks in chapter 93).

1 And after that Enoch both gave and began to recount from the books. And Enoch said:

2 'Concerning the children of righteousness and concerning the elect of the world, and concerning the plant of righteousness, I will speak these things. I Enoch will declare (them) to you, my sons, according to that which appeared to me in heavenly vision, and which I have known through the word of the holy angels, and have learned from heavenly tablets.'

3 And Enoch began to recount from the books and said: 'I was born the seventh in the first week, able judgment and righteousness still endured.

(Author's note: Enoch was the seventh son. He was born in the beginning of the time line he is laying out.)

4 And after me there shall arise in the second week great wickedness, and deceit shall have sprung up; and in it there shall be the first end.

(Author's note: This is the rise of evil. The angels have fallen.)

5 And in it a man shall be saved; and after it is ended unrighteousness shall grow up, and a law shall be made for the sinners. And after that in the third week at its close a man shall be elected as the plant of righteous judgment, and his posterity shall become the plant of righteousness for evermore.

(Author's note: The time of Moses and the establishment of the Ten Commandments. The beginning of the law.)

6 And after that in the fourth week, at its close, visions of the holy and righteous shall be seen, and a law for all generations and an enclosure shall be made for them.

(Author's note: The time of David and the wars that defined the holy land.)

7 And after that in the fifth week, at its close, the house of glory and dominion shall be built for ever.

(Author's note: The time of Solomon and the first temple.)

8 And after that in the sixth week, all who live in it shall be blinded, and the hearts of all of them shall godlessly forsake wisdom. And in it a man shall ascend; and at its close the house of dominion shall be burned with fire, and the whole race of the chosen root shall be dispersed.

(Author's note: In the sixth week Christ came to the chosen ones, but they were blinded. He ascended and the Jewish nation was scattered. In the holocaust innumerable Jews were burned. The Diaspora remains scattered but has begun to gather into the new nation of Israel.)

9 And after that in the seventh week shall an apostate generation arise, and many shall be its deeds, and all its deeds shall be apostate.

(Author's note: It is assumed that we are in the seventh week of Enoch's prophecy. This aligns in a very general way to the prophecies of the churches in Revelation. At the end of the seventh week there will be a "great falling away." This is cited in the Holy Bible in the book of 2 Thessalonians and Revelation. Here are the related scriptures.)

2 Thessalonians 2:3 Let no man deceive you by any means: for that day shall not come, except there come a falling away first, and that man of sin be revealed, the son of perdition;

Revelation 2
1 Unto the angel of the church of Ephesus write; These things saith he that holdeth the seven stars in his right hand, who walketh in the midst of the seven golden candlesticks;
2 I know thy works, and thy labour, and thy patience, and how thou canst not bear them which are evil: and thou hast tried them which say they are apostles, and are not, and hast found them liars:
3 And hast borne, and hast patience, and for my name's sake hast laboured, and hast not fainted.
4 Nevertheless I have somewhat against thee, because thou hast left thy first love.
5 Remember therefore from whence thou art fallen, and repent, and do the first works; or else I will come unto thee quickly, and will remove thy candlestick out of his place, except thou repent.
6 But this thou hast, that thou hatest the deeds of the

Nicolaitanes, which I also hate.

7 He that hath an ear, let him hear what the Spirit saith unto the churches; To him that overcometh will I give to eat of the tree of life, which is in the midst of the paradise of God.

8 And unto the angel of the church in Smyrna write; These things saith the first and the last, which was dead, and is alive;

9 I know thy works, and tribulation, and poverty, (but thou art rich) and I know the blasphemy of them which say they are Jews, and are not, but are the synagogue of Satan.

10 Fear none of those things which thou shalt suffer: behold, the devil shall cast some of you into prison, that ye may be tried; and ye shall have tribulation ten days: be thou faithful unto death, and I will give thee a crown of life.

11 He that hath an ear, let him hear what the Spirit saith unto the churches; He that overcometh shall not be hurt of the second death.

12 And to the angel of the church in Pergamos write; These things saith he which hath the sharp sword with two edges;

13 I know thy works, and where thou dwellest, even where Satan's seat is: and thou holdest fast my name, and hast not denied my faith, even in those days wherein Antipas was my faithful martyr, who was slain among you, where Satan dwelleth.

14 But I have a few things against thee, because thou hast there them that hold the doctrine of Balaam, who taught Balac to cast a stumblingblock before the children of Israel, to eat things sacrificed unto idols, and to commit fornication.

15 So hast thou also them that hold the doctrine of the Nicolaitanes, which thing I hate.

16 Repent; or else I will come unto thee quickly, and will fight against them with the sword of my mouth.

17 He that hath an ear, let him hear what the Spirit saith unto the churches; To him that overcometh will I give to eat of the hidden manna, and will give him a white stone, and in the stone a new name written, which no man knoweth saving he that receiveth it.

18 And unto the angel of the church in Thyatira write; These things saith the Son of God, who hath his eyes like unto a flame of fire, and his feet are like fine brass;

19 I know thy works, and charity, and service, and faith, and thy patience, and thy works; and the last to be more than the first.

20 Notwithstanding I have a few things against thee, because thou sufferest that woman Jezebel, which calleth herself a prophetess, to teach and to seduce my servants to commit fornication, and to eat things sacrificed unto idols.

21 And I gave her space to repent of her fornication; and she repented not.

22 Behold, I will cast her into a bed, and them that

commit adultery with her into great tribulation, except they repent of their deeds.

23 And I will kill her children with death; and all the churches shall know that I am he which searcheth the reins and hearts: and I will give unto every one of you according to your works.

24 But unto you I say, and unto the rest in Thyatira, as many as have not this doctrine, and which have not known the depths of Satan, as they speak; I will put upon you none other burden.

25 But that which ye have already hold fast till I come.

26 And he that overcometh, and keepeth my works unto the end, to him will I give power over the nations:

27 And he shall rule them with a rod of iron; as the vessels of a potter shall they be broken to shivers: even as I received of my Father.

28 And I will give him the morning star.

29 He that hath an ear, let him hear what the Spirit saith unto the churches.

Revelation 3

1 And unto the angel of the church in Sardis write; These things saith he that hath the seven Spirits of God, and the seven stars; I know thy works, that thou hast a name that thou livest, and art dead.

2 Be watchful, and strengthen the things which remain, that are ready to die: for I have not found thy works perfect before God.

3 *Remember therefore how thou hast received and heard, and hold fast, and repent. If therefore thou shalt not watch, I will come on thee as a thief, and thou shalt not know what hour I will come upon thee.*

4 *Thou hast a few names even in Sardis which have not defiled their garments; and they shall walk with me in white: for they are worthy.*

5 *He that overcometh, the same shall be clothed in white raiment; and I will not blot out his name out of the book of life, but I will confess his name before my Father, and before his angels.*

6 *He that hath an ear, let him hear what the Spirit saith unto the churches.*

7 *And to the angel of the church in Philadelphia write; These things saith he that is holy, he that is true, he that hath the key of David, he that openeth, and no man shutteth; and shutteth, and no man openeth;*

8 *I know thy works: behold, I have set before thee an open door, and no man can shut it: for thou hast a little strength, and hast kept my word, and hast not denied my name.*

9 *Behold, I will make them of the synagogue of Satan, which say they are Jews, and are not, but do lie; behold, I will make them to come and worship before thy feet, and to know that I have loved thee.*

10 *Because thou hast kept the word of my patience, I also will keep thee from the hour of temptation, which*

shall come upon all the world, to try them that dwell upon the earth.

11 Behold, I come quickly: hold that fast which thou hast, that no man take thy crown.

12 Him that overcometh will I make a pillar in the temple of my God, and he shall go no more out: and I will write upon him the name of my God, and the name of the city of my God, which is new Jerusalem, which cometh down out of heaven from my God: and I will write upon him my new name.

(Author's note: Most scholars agree that we are in the age of Laodicea)

13 He that hath an ear, let him hear what the Spirit saith unto the churches.

14 And unto the angel of the church of the Laodiceans write; These things saith the Amen, the faithful and true witness, the beginning of the creation of God;

15 I know thy works, that thou art neither cold nor hot: I would thou wert cold or hot.

16 So then because thou art lukewarm, and neither cold nor hot, I will spue thee out of my mouth.

17 Because thou sayest, I am rich, and increased with goods, and have need of nothing; and knowest not that thou art wretched, and miserable, and poor, and blind, and naked:

18 I counsel thee to buy of me gold tried in the fire, that

thou mayest be rich; and white raiment, that thou
mayest be clothed, and that the shame of thy nakedness
do not appear; and anoint thine eyes with eyesalve, that
thou mayest see.

19 As many as I love, I rebuke and chasten: be zealous
therefore, and repent.

20 Behold, I stand at the door, and knock: if any man
hear my voice, and open the door, I will come in to him,
and will sup with him, and he with me.

21 To him that overcometh will I grant to sit with me in
my throne, even as I also overcame, and am set down
with my Father in his throne.

22 He that hath an ear, let him hear what the Spirit
saith unto the churches.

(Picking up from the Book of Enoch.)

10 And at its end shall be elected, the elect
righteous of the eternal plant of righteousness
shall be chosen to receive sevenfold instruction
concerning all His creation.

11 For who is there of all the children of men that
is able to hear the voice of the Holy One without
being troubled? And who can think His
thoughts? Who is there that can behold all the
works of heaven?

12 And how should there be one who could behold heaven, and who is there that could understand the things of heaven and see a soul or a spirit and could tell of it, or ascend and see all their ends and think them or do like them?

13 And who is there of all men that could know what is the breadth and the length of the earth, and to whom has the measurement been shown of all of them?

14 Or is there any one who could discern the length of the heaven and how great is its height, and on what it is founded, and how great is the number of stars, and where the luminaries rest?

Chapter Three
The War Scroll Symbols

Now, let us look carefully at the War Scroll. This scroll describes a seven stage confrontation between the "Sons of Light" under the leadership of the "Prince of Light", also called Michael, the Archangel – and the "Sons of Darkness", aided by a nation called the Kittim, led by the evil deity, Belial.

Kittim - was a settlement in present-day Larnaca on the west coast of Cyprus, known in ancient times as Kition, or (in Latin) Citium. On this basis, the whole island became known as "Kittim" in Hebrew, including the Hebrew Bible. However the name seems to have been employed with some flexibility in Hebrew literature. The expression "isles of Kittim", found in the Book of Jeremiah 2:10 and Ezekiel 27:6, indicates that, some centuries prior to Josephus, this designation had already become a general descriptor for the Mediterranean islands. Sometimes this designation was further extended to apply to Romans, Macedonians or Seleucid Greeks. The Septuagint translates the occurrence of "Kittim" in the Book of Daniel 11:30 as ῥωμαῖοι ("Romans"). 1 Maccabees 1:1 states that "Alexander the Great the Macedonian" had come from the "land of Kittim." In the War of the Sons of

Light Against the Sons of Darkness from the Dead Sea Scrolls, the people of Kittim are referred to as being "of Asshur". Eleazar Sukenik argued that this reference to Asshur should be understood to refer to the Seleucid Empire which controlled the territory of the former Assyrian Empire at that time, but his son Yigael Yadin interpreted this phrase as a veiled reference to the Romans.

Although Kittim is singled out as the most evil and vile, other nations and peoples are mentioned specifically as the enemies of God. In the first paragraph of the text we read: "The troops are from Edom, Moab, the sons of Ammon, the Amalekites, Philistia, and the troops of the Kittim of Asshur. Supporting them are those who have violated the covenant. "

Edom - Genesis 25:30 King James Version (KJV)
30 "And Esau said to Jacob, Feed me, I pray thee, with that same red pottage; for I am faint: therefore was his name called Edom." The name Edom means "red" in Hebrew, and was given to Esau, the elder son of the Hebrew patriarch Isaac, once he ate the "red pottage", which the Bible used in irony at the fact he was born "red all over", likely meaning he had red hair. The Torah, Tanakh and New Testament thus describe the Edomites as

79

descendants of Esau. Malachi 1 sums up the view of Israel toward the descendents of Essau. "I Loved Jacob, but Esau I Hated"

1 This is a divine revelation. The Lord spoke his word to Israel through Malachi.
2 "I loved you," says the Lord.
"But you ask, 'How did you love us?'
"Wasn't Esau Jacob's brother?" declares the Lord. "I loved Jacob, 3 but Esau I hated. I turned his mountains into a wasteland and left his inheritance to the jackals in the desert.
4 "The descendants of Esau may say, 'We have been beaten down, but we will rebuild the ruins.'
"Yet, this is what the Lord of Armies says: They may rebuild, but I will tear it down. They will be called 'the Wicked Land' and 'the people with whom the Lord is always angry.' 5 You will see these things with your own eyes and say, 'Even outside the borders of Israel the Lord is great."

In the time of Nebuchadnezzar II the Edomites helped plunder Jerusalem and slaughter the Judaeans. For this reason the Prophets denounced Edom violently.

Moab – The incestuous pairing of Lot and his daughter produced Moab and spawned a people who were considered at one time to be "cousins" of the Jews. However, as customs and kingdoms diverged, trouble and disputes set in. At the disruption of the kingdom under the reign of Rehoboam, Moab seems to have been absorbed into the Northern Kingdom In about 853 BCE the Moabites refused to pay tribute and asserted their independence, making war upon the kingdom of Judah. After the death of Ahab in about 853 BCE, the Moabites under Mesha rebelled against Jehoram, who continued the military stance of his father, Jehoshaphat, King of the Kingdom of Judah, and with the King of Edom. In the year of Elisha's death they invaded Israel and later aided Nebuchadnezzar in his expedition against Jehoiakim. Moab had contempt for Israel.

Jehoshaphat ascended the throne at the age of thirty-five and reigned for twenty-five years. He spent the first years of his reign fortifying his kingdom against the Kingdom of Israel. He stopped idolatrous practices in the "high places" according to 2 Chronicles 17:6. In the third year of his reign, Jehoshaphat sent out priests and Levites over the land to instruct the people in the Law, an activity that was commanded for a Sabbatical year (7 year cycle) in Deuteronomy 31:10-31:13). The author of Books of Chronicles states that the kingdom enjoyed a great measure of peace and prosperity, the blessing of God resting on the people "in their basket and their store."

Jehoram of Judah was a king of Judah, and the son of Jehoshaphat. Jehoram took the throne at the age of 32 and reigned for 8 years. (2 Kings 8:17)
William F. Albright has dated his reign to 849 – 842 BC.

Ammon - According to the biblical account, Ammon was born to Lot's younger daughter and Moab was born to Lot's elder daughter, in the aftermath of the destruction of Sodom and Gomorrah, when the daughter believed they were the only people left on earth and hastily set up a plan to repopulate the earth by sleeping with there father, whom they had gotten intoxicated. The Bible refers to both the Ammonites and Moabites as the "children of Lot". Genesis 19:37-38. The Hebrew tradition makes this tribe related to the Israelites. Hence the Israelites are commanded to avoid conflict with them on their march to the Promised Land (Deuteronomy 2:19).
Ammonites and Israelites did not have an enduring friendship. Like the Moabites, they are considered a

lower class. During the Exodus, the Israelites were prohibited by the Ammonites from passing through their lands. In the Book of Judges, the Ammonites worked with Eglon, king of the Moabites against Israel. Attacks by the Ammonites on Israelite communities east of the Jordan were the impetus behind the unification of the tribes under Saul, who convinced the tribes that their defense and conquest of these mutual foes were more important than their petty in-fighting. The Ammonites and Moabites displayed hostility to both kingdoms, Judah and Israel, in what seemed to be never-ending skirmishes.

Amalekites - The Amalekites were a people mentioned a number of times in the book of Genesis, and considered to be Amalek's descendants. In the chant of Balaam in Numbers, 24:20, Amalek was called the 'first of the nations', attesting to its antiquity.

The name Amalek's etymology traces as a people who lick blood. This act could refer to cannibalism but is it much more likely refers to the fact that the consuming of blood is forbidden under Jewish law, making this nation an abomination in the Jewish view point.

The Arabic language seems to have originated with the Amalekites. Gen. 14:7 may indicate the Amalekites existed as early as the time of Abraham, in the region that would later become the Roman province of Arabia Petraea. In the Pentateuch, the Amalekites are nomads who attacked the Hebrews at Rephidim (Exodus 17:8-10) in the desert of Sinai during their exodus from Egypt: "smiting the hindmost, all that were feeble behind," (Deuteronomy 25:18). Saul and his army destroyed most of the people, and earned Samuel's wrath for leaving some of the people and livestock alive (1 Samuel 15:8-9) against God's command. Saul and the tribal leaders also hesitated to kill Agag, so Samuel himself executed the Amalekite king (1 Samuel 15:33).

David waged a sacred war of extermination against the Amalekites, who may have subsequently disappeared from history.

Amalekite tribes without provocation pounced on the Hebrews when they were weak. The Amalekites became associated with ruthlessness and trickery and tyranny, even more so than Pharaoh or the Philistines, and required a ruthless response:

Ex 17: 8 Then Amalek came and fought with Israel at Rephidim. So Moses said to Joshua, "Choose for us men, and go out and fight with Amalek. Tomorrow I will stand on the top of the hill with the staff of God in my hand." 10 So Joshua did as Moses told him, and fought with Amalek, while Moses, Aaron, and Hur went up to the top of the hill. 11 Whenever Moses held up his hand, Israel prevailed, and whenever he lowered his hand, Amalek prevailed. 12 But Moses' hands grew weary, so they took a stone and put it under him, and he sat on it, while Aaron and Hur held up his hands, one on one side, and the other on the other side. So his hands were steady until the going down of the sun. 13 And Joshua overwhelmed Amalek and his people with the sword.

14 Then the Lord said to Moses, "Write this as a memorial in a book and recite it in the ears of Joshua, that I will utterly blot out the memory of Amalek from under heaven." 15 And Moses built an altar and called the name of it, The Lord is my banner, 16 saying, "A hand upon the throne of the Lord Jacob! The Lord will have war with Amalek from generation to generation."

Philistia - Philistia was a Pentapolis (5 city-state configuation) in south-western Levant, comprising

Ashkelon, Ashdod, Ekron, Gath, and Gaza, established by migrant tribes called the Philistines, c.1175 BCE. They were in constant struggle with the neighboring Egyptians, Israelites, and Canaanites, but in time and through exposure they gradually absorbed most of the Canaanite culture. Philistia was eventually conquered and subdued by neighboring Israelites. The Bible portrays them as one of the Kingdom of Israel's most dangerous enemies.

The prophet Amos tells us:
...Have not I brought up Israel out of the land of Egypt? and the Philistines from Caphtor... (Amos 9.7).

Another clue as to their origins is in the book of Genesis. In the tenth chapter we find the family tree of the sons of Noah - Shem, Ham and Japheth. From Shem descended the Semitic peoples and in due course the sons of Jacob, the Israelites. The descendants of Ham traveled and settled in Egypt to replenish and populate the earth after the Flood. It is from Ham that the Philistines' lineage can be traced:

Now these are the generations of the sons of Noah, Shem, Ham, and Japheth: and unto them were sons born after the flood. ...And the sons of Ham...And Mizraim begat Ludim, and Anamim, and Lehabim, and Naphtuhim, and Pathrusim, and Casluhim, (out of whom came Philistim,) and Caphtorim.' (Genesis 10.1,6,13,14)

Asshur – This may be another name for Assyria. Ashur was the son of Shem and is sometimes compared with the figure of the deity Ashur, for whom a temple was dedicated in the early capital city of Aššur by an Assyrian king named Ushpia, ca. 21st century BC. The city and the Assyrian nation and people, were named in honor of this deity.

In the War Scroll we observe a typical religious binary outlook on the world where God is on the side of the writer and his people and all who oppose the standards set by the originators of the text and his or her people are considered evil. In such a fundamental religious outlook there is no gray area. Everything is black or white. We see this playing out still in 2014 AD at the writing of this book in the same areas of the Middle East. The religious zealots of Islam called ISIL are slaughtering and beheading innocent civilians, women, and children, because they do not belong to the same sect of their religion. Thus, in such an environment one needs to demonize the perceived enemy before killing them. This is done through labels and terms. This point is driven home by the mindset of the members of the Qumran Community since they use the term, "Sons of Darkness" to refer to all non-Jew and any Jew that does not meet their measurement of piety.

The term, Son's of Light" is used by Community members to refer to themselves. It seems a standard behavior for armies to assume they are unquestionably in the right and on the side of God when marching into war.

A pure and powerful army must have a pure and powerful leader. In this case, it is not the Messiah but the Archangel Michael, the general of the army of God and leader of the Sons of Light.

Likewise, any evil army must have an evil leader. Belial leads the Sons of Darkness. The name, Belial means "worthless" or "without value." The War Scroll and the Thanksgiving Hymns both put forth the idea that Belial is accursed by God, but God allows Belial to persist as a way to separate the good from the bad and to purify those who are good through their trials.

In the Dead Sea Scrolls, Belial is further contrasted with God. These are the Angel of Light and the Angel of Darkness. The Manual of Discipline identifies the Angel of Light as God himself. The Angel of Darkness is identified in the same scroll as Belial. Thus, in this context the modern reader could identify Belial with a type of Satan.

Also in The Dead Sea Scrolls is a recounting of a dream of Amram, the father of Moses, who finds two Watchers contesting over him. One is Belial who is described as the King of Evil and Prince of Darkness. This narrative indicates Belial is a fallen or rebellious angel.

Belial is also mentioned in the Fragments of a Zadokite Work, which is also known as The Damascus Document. In the text, "Belial shall be let loose against Israel, as God spoke through Isaiah the prophet." This event is to happen during the eschatological age. The Fragments also speak of "three nets of Belial" which are said to be fornication, wealth, and pollution of the sanctuary. In this work, Belial is sometimes presented as an agent of divine punishment and sometimes as a rebel. The Book of Jubilees labels all uncircumcised gentiles as the sons of Belial.

The writer of the War Scroll relies heavily on the mystical symbolism of numbers. The confrontation between the army of Darkness and the army of Light would last 49 years, terminating in the victory of the "Sons of Light" and the restoration of the Temple service and sacrifices. This would indicate that the services and sacrifices were already interrupted and were a point of great concern to the writers at Qumran.

The length of the time, 49 years, is significant. It is 7 times 7 and is the span between Jubilees, which occurs every 50 years.

The Jubilee (Hebrew yovel יובל) year is the year at the end of seven cycles of shmita. The sabbath year, or shmita is a Hebrew word meaning "release". It is also called the sabbatical year or sheviit , which is Hebrew for "seventh" and is the seventh year of the seven-year agricultural cycle mandated by the Torah for the Land of Israel, and still observed in contemporary Judaism. Sabbatical years, according to Biblical regulations, had a special impact on the ownership and management of land in the Land of Israel. There is some debate whether it was the 49th year (the last year of seven sabbatical cycles, referred to as the Sabbath's Sabbath), or whether it was the following (50th) year. Jubilee deals largely with land, property, and property rights. According to Leviticus, slaves and prisoners would be freed, debts would be forgiven and the mercies of God would be particularly manifest. Leviticus 25:8-13 states:

"And thou shalt number seven sabbaths of years unto thee, seven times seven years; and the space of the seven sabbaths of years shall be unto thee forty and nine years. Then shalt thou cause the trumpet of the jubilee to sound on the tenth day of the seventh month, in the day of atonement shall ye make the trumpet sound throughout all your land. And ye shall hallow the fiftieth year, and proclaim liberty throughout all the land unto all the inhabitants thereof: it shall be a jubilee unto you; and ye shall return every man unto his possession, and ye shall return every man unto his family. A jubilee shall that fiftieth year be unto you: ye shall not sow, neither reap that which groweth of itself in it, nor gather the grapes in it of thy vine undressed. For it is the jubilee; it shall be holy unto you: ye shall eat the increase thereof out of the field. In the year of this jubilee ye shall return every man unto his possession."

The biblical rules concerning Sabbatical years (shmita) are still observed by many religious Jews in the State of Israel, but the regulations for the Jubilee year have not been observed for many centuries.

In Hebrew symbolism the number 7 indicates divine perfection, or a completeness that is sacred. When numbers are repeated, such as 7 times 7 it is to make a point of the power or meaning of the underlying number. The number may be hidden within a text by splitting the numbers. For example, if the number 52 appears it is also an indication of 7 since 5 plus 2 equals 7. We would examine the meanings of 5 and 2, which was used to make up the mystical number 7, which would be the sum. Other such numbers are mentioned, which we will examine within the text.

The War Scroll describes battle arrays, weaponry, the ages of the participants, and military maneuvers, recalling Hellenistic and Roman military manuals.

The scroll is a mixture of warfare and law or rule. All things in the community seem to be codified and ritualized in form and fashion, even battles. Since the battle is pre-scripted, there has been thought given to the symbolism of names, engraved phrases upon weapons, and numbers.

Jewish sacred writings make use of such symbolism and the War Scroll is no exception.

In this battle, consisting of a number of engagements, there is also a ritualized fashion of engagement in which the Sons of Light are pure and obedient to the laws and rules of the community and thus will perform their duties as warriors exactly as instructed by the priests. Because of their piety, when faced with evil God will intervene, conquer, and save his people.

In this scenario one sees clear parallels to the books of Ezekiel, Revelation, Daniel, and Enoch, along with other biblical texts. Indeed, some assume the author borrowed from Daniel as well as other material of the day, according to the date of the text's creation. All three books, Daniel, Revelations, and the War Scroll, share the common theme of life and light being victorious over evil and death. All point to the fact that the outcome is already known, however, man must participate and persevere, and is thus held culpable in the outcome.

Chapter Four

The War Scroll
The Battle of the Sons of Light
and the Sons of Darkness

Authors notes, supporting Bible scriptures, and commentary are placed within the text in italics. If the text is missing or unreadable it is indicated with (...).

The War Scroll

The Master Rule of War.

The first attack of the Sons of Light will be initiated against the forces of the Sons of Darkness, which is the army of Belial. The troops are from Edom, Moab, the sons of Ammon, the Amalekites, Philistia, and the troops of the Kittim of Asshur. Supporting them are those who have violated the covenant.

The sons of Levi, the sons of Judah, and the sons of Benjamin, and those exiled to the wilderness, will fight against them with (...) against all their troops, when the exiles of the Sons of Light return from the Wilderness of the Peoples to camp in the Wilderness of Jerusalem.

Ten of the original twelve Hebrew tribes under the leadership of Joshua took possession of Canaan, the Promised Land, after the death of Moses. They were named Asher, Dan, Ephraim, Gad, Issachar, Manasseh,

95

Naphtali, Reuben, Simeon, and Zebulun — all sons or grandsons of Jacob. In 930 BCE the ten tribes formed the independent Kingdom of Israel in the north. The two other tribes, Judah and Benjamin, formed the Kingdom of Judah in the south. Following the conquest of the northern kingdom by the Assyrians in 721 BCE, the ten tribes were gradually assimilated by other peoples and thus disappeared from history. It is the belief held by many Jews that the ten tribes will come back and the tribes will be united in the time of the return of the Messiah.

Then after the battle they will go up from that place and battle the king of the Kittim and he shall enter into Egypt. In his time he will go out with great anger to do battle against the kings of the north, and in his anger he shall set out to destroy and eliminate the strength of Israel.

Then there will be a time of salvation for the People of God, and a time of the dominion of all the men of His forces, and a time of eternal destruction for all the forces of Belial. There shall be great panic among the sons of Japheth, and Assyria shall fall with no one to come to his aid, and the supremacy of the Kittim shall cease their wickedness and will be overcome without a single survivor. There shall be no survivors of all the Sons of Darkness.

Japheth was one of the three sons of Noah. The descendants of Japheth occupied the "isles of the Gentiles," (Genesis 10:5) which are the coast lands of the Mediterranean Sea in Europe and Asia Minor. From there they spread northward over the whole continent of Europe and a considerable portion of Asia.

Genesis 10:5 NIV New Living Translation
Their descendants became the seafaring peoples that spread out to various lands, each identified by its own language, clan, and national identity.

Assyria was a kingdom of northern Mesopotamia that became the centre of one of the great empires of the ancient Middle East. It was located in what is now northern Iraq and southeastern Turkey.

In Genesis 10:4 the word is applied to the descendants of Javan, and indicates, therefore, the Greek-Latin races, whose territory extended along the coasts of the Mediterranean, and included its islands. It is generally explained as Cyprus in a narrow definition or Sicily with Southern Italy, Spain and Rhodes in a broader sense.

The statement of Josephus, that "all islands, and the greatest part of the sea-coast, are called Chethim (Kittim) by the Hebrews," on the other hand, must be taken as the testimony of one well acquainted with the opinions of the learned world in his time. In Jeremiah 2:10 and Ezekiel 27:6 the isles of Kittim are expressly spoken of, and this confirms the statement of Josephus concerning the extended meaning of the name. This would explain its application to the Roman fleet in Daniel 11:30 (so the Vulgate), and the Macedonians in 1 Macc 1:1 (Chettieim) and 8:5 (Kitians). In the latter passage the Greek writer seems to have been thinking more of the Cyprian Kition than of the Hebrew Kittim.

Then the Sons of Righteousness shall shine into all ends of the world and continuing to shine forth until end of the appointed seasons of darkness. Then at the time appointed by God, His great brilliance will shine for all of eternity for the peace and blessing, glory and joy, and long life of all Sons of Light. On the day when the Kittim falls there will be a battle and horrible carnage before the God of Israel, for it is a day appointed by Him from ancient times as a battle of destruction for the Sons of Darkness.

On that day the congregation of the gods and the congregation of men shall engage one another and the outcome will be great carnage. The Sons of Light and the forces of Darkness shall fight one another to show the strength of God with the roar of a great multitude and the shout of gods and men. It will be a day of disaster. It is a time of distress for all the people who are redeemed by God. Compared to all their afflictions, no day exists like this and it is hastening to its completion as an eternal redemption. On the day of their battle against the Kittim, they shall go out to kill in battle.

The statement regarding the "congregation of the gods" may point to angles being called elohim or it may point to Psalms 82.

Psalm 82 New International Version (NIV)
A psalm of Asaph.

1 God presides in the great assembly;
 he renders judgment among the "gods":
2 "How long will you[a] defend the unjust
 and show partiality to the wicked?[b]
3 Defend the weak and the fatherless;
 uphold the cause of the poor and the oppressed.
4 Rescue the weak and the needy;
 deliver them from the hand of the wicked.
5 "The 'gods' know nothing, they understand nothing.
 They walk about in darkness;
 all the foundations of the earth are shaken.
6 "I said, 'You are "gods";

> *you are all sons of the Most High.'*
> *7 But you will die like mere mortals;*
> *you will fall like every other ruler."*
> *8 Rise up, O God, judge the earth,*
> *for all the nations are your inheritance.*

In three groups the Sons of Light will stand firm to strike a blow at wickedness, and in three (parts) the army of Belial shall strengthen themselves to force the retreat of the forces of Light.

The number three signifies spiritual completion or completeness.

And when the banners of the infantry cause their hearts to melt, then the power of God will strengthen the hearts of the Sons of Light.

In the seventh section, the great hand of God will overcome Belial and all the angels under his control, and all the men of his forces shall be destroyed forever. And this is the total destruction of the Sons of Darkness and service to God during the years of war.

Seven symbolizes spiritual perfection. Cycles of seven are sacred. The seventh day, or Sabbath is the day of rest and sacred to the Lord. The seven year cycles is the Shmita also called the Sabbath year, in which the land is supposed to rest. Seven Shmitas leads to the seven periods of seven years and on the fiftieth year occurs the Jubilee.

And the holy ones shall shine forth in support of the truth in the annihilation of the Sons of Darkness. Then a great roar (proceeded them when) they took hold of the implements of war. (And the) chiefs of the tribes and the priests, of the tribe of the Levites, the chiefs of the tribes, the fathers of the congregation, the priests and thus for the Levites and the courses of the heads (of the procession will go forth.)

The number of the congregation's tribe (family) is fifty-two. They shall set in the rank the chiefs of the priests after the Chief Priest and his deputy. There will be twelve chief priests to serve in the regular offering before God. The chiefs of the courses will number twenty-six and shall serve in their courses. After them the chiefs of the Levites who serve continually will number twelve in all, one to a tribe. The chiefs of their courses shall serve each man in his office. The chiefs of the tribes and fathers of the congregation shall support them, taking their posts continually at the gates of the sanctuary.

In occurrences of multi-digit numbers, the individual digits are examined as part of the whole. The digits are added together to get a single digit, which carries a spiritual meaning. In the case of the number "52" the two digits are 5 and 2. Five is the number of grace and the spirit of God. Two is the number of cooperation, partnership and witnessing. Together the digits add up to seven, which is the number of spiritual perfection.

The number twelve is significant in and of itself, without reduction. It is the number of government perfected. It is the symbol of theocracy; a government overseen and arranged by God. There were twelve tribes, twelve apostles who will sit in judgment over the tribes, and twelve gates into the holy city when it descends. When reduced, the number twelve comes back to the holy number three.

The chiefs of their courses, from the age of fifty upwards, shall take their posts with their commissioners on their festivals, which are new moons and Sabbaths, and on every day of the year. These shall take their posts at the burnt offerings and sacrifices, to arrange the sweet smelling incense according to the will of God, in order to atone for all His congregation, and to satisfy themselves before Him continually at the table of glory. All of these they shall arrange at the time of the year of remission.

Fifty is used approximately three hundred times in the Bible. The number fifty points to deliverance and restoration following seven cycles of seven years.

According to Leviticus 25:8-55, special instruction was given concerning the fiftieth year. It was the year for the Israelites to rejoice and be jubilant. Therefore, the fiftieth year is known as the Year of Jubilee when the Israelites were told to "proclaim liberty throughout all the land."

Fifty is also the number of salvation. In Genesis 18, Abraham's prayer was for God to spare wicked Sodom if fifty righteous people were found there. The base number of fifty is five, which is the number of the spirit of God and His grace.

During the remaining thirty-three years of the war the men of renown, those called of the Congregation, and all the heads of the congregation's family shall choose for themselves men of war for all the lands of the nations.

The number 33 reduces to 6. (3+3=6) Six is the number for man because he was created on the sixth day. It is the highest and lowest man can achieve. It is the number of family because Adam and Eve were created together on the sixth day. It should remind us of our human incompleteness. Six will always fall one below the perfect number seven. The sixth commandment calls our attention to the value of the human life that was created on the sixth day. It says, "Do not kill" (Exodus 20:13).

They shall prepare capable men for themselves from all tribes of Israel to go out for battle according to the call to war (draft), year by year. But during the years of remission they shall not ready men to go out for battle, for it is a Sabbath of rest for Israel.

The war will be waged during the thirty-five years of service. For six years the entire congregation will wage it together. Then the war shall be waged with divisions during the twenty-nine remaining years.

The number 35 reduces to 8. Eight is the number of the law and justice. Circumcisions took place on the eighth day, symbolizing being placed under the law of God. According to E.W. Bullinger in his book, "Numbers in Scripture," the number eight also represents strength and health.

In the first year they will fight against Mesopotamia. In the second the war will be fought against the sons of Lud. In the third they shall fight against the rest of the sons of Aram, which are Uz, Hul, Togar, and Mesha, who are beyond the

Euphrates. In the fourth and fifth years they will battle against the sons of Arpachshad. In the sixth and seventh year they shall fight against all the sons of Assyria and Persia and those of the east up to the Great Desert. In the eighth year they will fight against the sons of Elam. In the ninth year they will fight against the sons of Ishmael and Keturah. And during the following ten years the war shall be divided against all the sons of Ham according to their families (tribes/clans) and their territories. During the remaining ten years the war shall be divided against all sons of Japheth according to their territories.

The entire war is made up of various battles, which will last for 35 years. A Six Year War will be waged by the entire congregation

Twenty-nine years of war remains, which will be waged with various divisions of the army. The following list breaks down the timeframe from the first engagement to the last attack.

Year 0-1	*Mesopotania*
Year 1-2	*Lud*
Year 2-3	*Aram (Uz, Hul, Togar, Mesha)*
Years 3-5	*Arpachsad*
Years 5-7	*Assyria, Persia*

Year 7-8	Elam
Year 8-9	Islmael, Keturah
Years 9-19	Ham's descendants
Years 19-29	Japheth's descendants

With the first 6 year war, plus the 29 years of targeted incursions, the entire crusade will last 35 years.

Mesopotamia *(from the Greek, meaning 'between two rivers') was an ancient region in the eastern Mediterranean bounded in the northeast by the Zagros Mountains and in the southeast by the Arabian Plateau, corresponding to today's Iraq, mostly, but also parts of modern-day Iran, Syria and Turkey. The 'two rivers' referred to in the name are the Tigris and the Euphrates rivers. The land between them was known as 'Al-Jazirah '(the island) by the Arabs. This area would later be called the "Fertile Crescent.*

The history, religion, and civilization of ***Persia*** *are offshoots from those of Media. Both Medes and Persians are Aryans. Aryans who settled in the southern part of the Iranian plateau became known as Persians, while those of the mountain regions of the northwest were called Medes. The Medes were at first the leading nation, but towards the middle of the sixth century, B.C. the Persians became the dominant power, not only in Iran, but also in Western Asia. Persia became the general* *name of the whole country formerly comprising Media, Susiana, Elam, and even Mesopotamia. What we now call Persia is not identical with the ancient empire designated by that name. That empire covered, from the sixth century B.C. to the seventh of our era, such vast regions as Persia proper, Media, Elam, Chaldea, Babylonia, Assyria, the highlands of Armenia and Bactriana, North-Eastern Arabia, and even Egypt. Persia proper is bounded on the north by Transcaucasia, the Caspian Sea, and Russian Turkestan; on the south by the Indian Ocean and the Persian Gulf, having an area of about 642,000 square miles.*

Lud *was a son of Shem and grandson of Noah.*
In the Book of Jubilees we read: "... until it reaches, toward the east, toward his brother **Asshur**'s *portion."*
Jubilees also says that **Japheth**'s *son Javan received islands in front of Lud's portion, and that Tubal received three large peninsulae, beginning with the first peninsula nearest Lud's portion. In all these cases, 'Lud's portion' seems to refer to the entire Anatolian peninsula, west of Mesopotamia.*

Some scholars have associated the Biblical **Lud** *with the Lubdu of Assyrian sources, who inhabited certain parts of western Media and Atropatene. It has been conjectured by others that Lud's descendants spread to areas of the far-east beyond Elam, or that they were* *identified with the Lullubi.*

The Muslim historian Muhammad ibn Jarir al-Tabari (c. 915) recounts a tradition that the wife of Lud was named Shakbah, daughter of Japheth, and that she bore him "Faris, Jurjan, and the races of Faris". He further asserts that Lud was the progenitor of not only the Persians, but also the **Amalekites** *and Canaanites, and all the peoples of the East, Oman, Hejaz,* **Syria, Egypt**, *and Bahrein.*

Aram *is a son of Shem, according to the Table of Nations in Genesis 10 of the Hebrew Bible, and the father* **of Uz, Hul,** *Gether and* **Mash**. *The Book of Chronicles confirms Aram as one of Shem's sons, confirming* **Uz, Hul,** *Gether and* **Mash**, *as also on the list of Shem's descendants. Aram son of Shem is recognized as a prophet in Mandaeism and as an Islamic prophet. Aram is usually regarded as being the eponymous ancestor of the Aramaean people of Northern Mesopotamia and Syria.*

Genesis 10 New International Version (NIV)
The Table of Nations
10 This is the account of Shem, Ham and Japheth, Noah's sons, who themselves had sons after the flood.
The Japhethites
2 The sons of **Japheth**: **Gomer, Magog**, *Madai, Javan, Tubal,* **Meshek** *and Tiras. 3 The sons of Gomer:*

Ashkenaz, Riphath and **Togarmah.**

4 The sons of Javan: Elishah, Tarshish, the Kittites and the Rodanites. 5 (From these the maritime peoples spread out into their territories by their clans within their nations, each with its own language.)

The Hamites

6 The sons of **Ham***: Cush, Egypt, Put and Canaan.*

7 The sons of Cush: Seba, Havilah, Sabtah, Raamah and Sabteka. The sons of Raamah: Sheba and Dedan. 8 Cush was the father of Nimrod, who became a mighty warrior on the earth. 9 He was a mighty hunter before the Lord; that is why it is said, "Like Nimrod, a mighty hunter before the Lord." 10 The first centers of his kingdom were Babylon, Uruk, Akkad and Kalneh, in Shinar. 11 From that land he went to **Assyria***, where he built Nineveh, Rehoboth Ir, Calah 12 and Resen, which is between Nineveh and Calah – which is the great city. 13 Egypt was the father of the* **Ludites, Anamites,** *Lehabites, Naphtuhites, 14 Pathrusites, Kasluhites (from whom the Philistines came) and Caphtorites. 15 Canaan was the father of Sidon his firstborn, and of the Hittites, 16 Jebusites, Amorites, Girgashites, 17 Hivites, Arkites, Sinites, 18 Arvadites, Zemarites and Hamathites. Later the Canaanite clans scattered 19 and the borders of Canaan reached from Sidon toward Gerar as far as Gaza, and then toward Sodom, Gomorrah, Admah and Zeboyim, as far as Lasha. 20 These are the sons of* **Ham** *by their clans and languages, in their territories and* nations.

The Semites

21 Sons were also born to Shem, whose older brother was **Japheth**; Shem was the ancestor of all the sons of Eber. 22 The sons of Shem: **Elam, Ashur, Arphaxad, Lud** and **Aram**. 23 The sons of Aram: **Uz, Hul**, Gether and **Meshek**. 24 Arphaxad was the father of Shelah, and Shelah the father of Eber. 25 Two sons were born to Eber: One was named Peleg, because in his time the earth was divided; his brother was named Joktan. 26 Joktan was the father of Almodad, Sheleph, Hazarmaveth, Jerah, 27 Hadoram, Uzal, Diklah, 28 Obal, Abimael, Sheba, 29 Ophir, Havilah and Jobab. All these were sons of Joktan. 30 The region where they lived stretched from **Mesha** toward Sephar, in the eastern hill country. 31 These are the sons of Shem by their clans and languages, in their territories and nations. 32 These are the clans of Noah's sons, according to their lines of descent, within their nations. From these the nations spread out over the earth after the flood.

Ezekiel 38 New International Version (NIV)
The Lord's Great Victory Over the Nations
38 The word of the Lord came to me: 2 "Son of man, set your face against **Gog, of the land of Magog**, the chief prince of Meshek and Tubal; prophesy against him 3 and

say: 'This is what the Sovereign Lord says: I am against you, **Gog**, chief prince of **Meshek** and Tubal. 4 I will turn you around, put hooks in your jaws and bring you out with your whole army – your horses, your horsemen fully armed, and a great horde with large and small shields, all of them brandishing their swords. 5 Persia, Cush and Put will be with them, all with shields and helmets, 6 also **Gomer** with all its troops, and **Beth Togarma**h from the far north with all its troops – the many nations with you.

7 "'Get ready; be prepared, you and all the hordes gathered about you, and take command of them. 8 After many days you will be called to arms. In future years you will invade a land that has recovered from war, whose people were gathered from many nations to the mountains of Israel, which had long been desolate. They had been brought out from the nations, and now all of them live in safety. 9 You and all your troops and the many nations with you will go up, advancing like a storm; you will be like a cloud covering the land.

10 "'This is what the Sovereign Lord says: On that day thoughts will come into your mind and you will devise an evil scheme. 11 You will say, "I will invade a land of unwalled villages; I will attack a peaceful and unsuspecting people – all of them living without walls and without gates and bars. 12 I will plunder and loot and turn my hand against the resettled ruins and the people gathered from the nations, rich in livestock and

goods, living at the center of the land.[d]" 13 Sheba and Dedan and the merchants of Tarshish and all her villages[e] will say to you, "Have you come to plunder? Have you gathered your hordes to loot, to carry off silver and gold, to take away livestock and goods and to seize much plunder?"'

14 "Therefore, son of man, prophesy and say to **Gog**: 'This is what the Sovereign Lord says: In that day, when my people Israel are living in safety, will you not take notice of it? 15 You will come from your place in the far north, you and many nations with you, all of them riding on horses, a great horde, a mighty army. 16 You will advance against my people Israel like a cloud that covers the land. In days to come, **Gog**, I will bring you against my land, so that the nations may know me when I am proved holy through you before their eyes.

17 "'This is what the Sovereign Lord says: You are the one I spoke of in former days by my servants the prophets of Israel. At that time they prophesied for years that I would bring you against them. 18 This is what will happen in that day: When **Gog** attacks the land of Israel, my hot anger will be aroused, declares the Sovereign Lord. 19 In my zeal and fiery wrath I declare that at that time there shall be a great earthquake in the land of Israel. 20 The fish in the sea, the birds in the sky, the beasts of the field, every creature that moves along the ground, and all the people on the face of the earth will tremble at my presence. The mountains will be

overturned, the cliffs will crumble and every wall will fall to the ground. 21 I will summon a sword against Gog on all my mountains, declares the Sovereign Lord. Every man's sword will be against his brother. 22 I will execute judgment on him with plague and bloodshed; I will pour down torrents of rain, hailstones and burning sulfur on him and on his troops and on the many nations with him. 23 And so I will show my greatness and my holiness, and I will make myself known in the sight of many nations. Then they will know that I am the Lord.'

Footnotes:

Ezekiel 38:2 Or the prince of Rosh,
Ezekiel 38:3 Or Gog, prince of Rosh,
Ezekiel 38:5 That is, the upper Nile region
Ezekiel 38:12 The Hebrew for this phrase means the navel of the earth.
Ezekiel 38:13 Or her strong lions

Ezekiel 39 New International Version (NIV)
39 "Son of man, prophesy against Gog and say: 'This is what the Sovereign Lord says: I am against you, Gog, chief prince of[a] Meshek and Tubal. 2 I will turn you around and drag you along. I will bring you from the far north and send you against the mountains of Israel. 3 Then I will strike your bow from your left hand and

*make your arrows drop from your right hand. 4 On the mountains of Israel you will fall, you and all your troops and the nations with you. I will give you as food to all kinds of carrion birds and to the wild animals. 5 You will fall in the open field, for I have spoken, declares the Sovereign Lord. 6 I will send fire on **Magog** and on those who live in safety in the coastlands, and they will know that I am the Lord.*

7 "'I will make known my holy name among my people Israel. I will no longer let my holy name be profaned, and the nations will know that I the Lord am the Holy One in Israel. 8 It is coming! It will surely take place, declares the Sovereign Lord. This is the day I have spoken of.

9 "'Then those who live in the towns of Israel will go out and use the weapons for fuel and burn them up — the small and large shields, the bows and arrows, the war clubs and spears. For seven years they will use them for fuel. 10 They will not need to gather wood from the fields or cut it from the forests, because they will use the weapons for fuel. And they will plunder those who plundered them and loot those who looted them, declares the Sovereign Lord.

*11 "'On that day I will give **Gog** a burial place in Israel, in the valley of those who travel east of the Sea. It will block the way of travelers, because Gog and all his hordes will be buried there. So it will be called the Valley of Hamon Gog.[b]*

12 "'For seven months the Israelites will be burying them in order to cleanse the land. 13 All the people of the land will bury them, and the day I display my glory will be a memorable day for them, declares the Sovereign Lord. 14 People will be continually employed in cleansing the land. They will spread out across the land and, along with others, they will bury any bodies that are lying on the ground.

"'After the seven months they will carry out a more detailed search. 15 As they go through the land, anyone who sees a human bone will leave a marker beside it until the gravediggers bury it in the Valley of Hamon **Gog***, 16 near a town called Hamonah. And so they will cleanse the land.'*

17 "Son of man, this is what the Sovereign Lord says: Call out to every kind of bird and all the wild animals: 'Assemble and come together from all around to the sacrifice I am preparing for you, the great sacrifice on the mountains of Israel. There you will eat flesh and drink blood. 18 You will eat the flesh of mighty men and drink the blood of the princes of the earth as if they were rams and lambs, goats and bulls — all of them fattened animals from Bashan. 19 At the sacrifice I am preparing for you, you will eat fat till you are glutted and drink blood till you are drunk. 20 At my table you will eat your fill of horses and riders, mighty men and soldiers of every kind,' declares the Sovereign Lord.

21 "I will display my glory among the nations, and all the nations will see the punishment I inflict and the hand I lay on them. 22 From that day forward the people of Israel will know that I am the Lord their God. 23 And the nations will know that the people of Israel went into exile for their sin, because they were unfaithful to me. So I hid my face from them and handed them over to their enemies, and they all fell by the sword. 24 I dealt with them according to their uncleanness and their offenses, and I hid my face from them.

25 "Therefore this is what the Sovereign Lord says: I will now restore the fortunes of Jacob[d] and will have compassion on all the people of Israel, and I will be zealous for my holy name. 26 They will forget their shame and all the unfaithfulness they showed toward me when they lived in safety in their land with no one to make them afraid. 27 When I have brought them back from the nations and have gathered them from the countries of their enemies, I will be proved holy through them in the sight of many nations. 28 Then they will know that I am the Lord their God, for though I sent them into exile among the nations, I will gather them to their own land, not leaving any behind. 29 I will no longer hide my face from them, for I will pour out my Spirit on the people of Israel, declares the Sovereign Lord."

Footnotes:

Ezekiel 39:1 Or Gog, prince of Rosh,
Ezekiel 39:11 Hamon Gog means hordes of Gog.
Ezekiel 39:16 Hamonah means horde.
Ezekiel 39:25 Or now bring Jacob back from captivity

Genesis 25 New International Version (NIV)
The Death of Abraham
1 Abraham had taken another wife, whose name was **Keturah.** *2 She bore him Zimran, Jokshan, Medan, Midian, Ishbak and Shuah. 3 Jokshan was the father of Sheba and Dedan; the descendants of Dedan were the Ashurites, the Letushites and the Leummites. 4 The sons of Midian were Ephah, Epher, Hanok, Abida and Eldaah. All these were descendants of* **Keturah.**

5 Abraham left everything he owned to Isaac. 6 But while he was still living, he gave gifts to the sons of his concubines and sent them away from his son Isaac to the land of the east.

7 Abraham lived a hundred and seventy-five years. 8 Then Abraham breathed his last and died at a good old age, an old man and full of years; and he was gathered to his people. 9 His sons Isaac and Ishmael buried him in the cave of Machpelah near Mamre, in the field of Ephron son of Zohar the Hittite, 10 the field Abraham had bought from the Hittites. There Abraham was buried with his wife Sarah. 11 After Abraham's death, God blessed his son Isaac, who then lived near Beer Lahai Roi.

Ishmael's Sons

12 This is the account of the family line of Abraham's son **Ishmael**, whom Sarah's slave, Hagar the Egyptian, bore to Abraham.

13 These are the names of the sons of **Ishmael**, listed in the order of their birth: Nebaioth the firstborn of Ishmael, Kedar, Adbeel, Mibsam, 14 Mishma, Dumah, Massa, 15 Hadad, Tema, Jetur, Naphish and Kedemah. 16 These were the sons of Ishmael, and these are the names of the twelve tribal rulers according to their settlements and camps. 17 Ishmael lived a hundred and thirty-seven years. He breathed his last and died, and he was gathered to his people. 18 His descendants settled in the area from Havilah to Shur, near the eastern border of Egypt, as you go toward Ashur. And they lived in hostility toward all the tribes related to them.

Gog and Magog have been associated with various individuals and places. Gog has been identified by modern scholars with Gyges, a 7th-century BCE king of Lydia, and with the Akkadian god Gaga. It has also been suggested that the name Magog is derived from an Akkadian word meaning "the land of Gyges." Magog may simple mean from or out of Gog since in the earlier *texts the phrases "Gog and Magog" is better rendered, "Out of Gog". In the 1st century CE the Jewish historian Josephus claimed that Gog and Magog were the Scythians, and in the 5th and 6th centuries they were held to be the Huns. Gog and Magog were equated with the Magyars in the 10th century and with the entire Muslim world, led by Muhammad and Saladin, in the Middle Ages. In both Jewish and Christian apocalyptic writings and other works, they were also identified with the Ten Lost Tribes of Israel.*

This is the Rule of the Trumpets:

These are the trumpets of alarm for all their service for the (armies of God) and their commissioned men, (The men will be set in divisions) by tens of thousands and thousands and hundreds and fifties and tens. Upon the trumpets (they will rely and upon the sounds of the trumpets, which) they shall (create for the different sounds of) the trumpets of the battle formations, and the trumpets for assembling them when the gates of the war are opened so that the infantry will advance, and the trumpets for the signal of the slain, and the trumpets of the ambush, and the trumpets of pursuit when the enemy is vanquished, and the trumpets of reassembly when the battle returns.

On the trumpets for the assembly of the

congregation they shall write, "The called of God."

On the trumpets for the assembly of the chiefs they shall write, "The princes of God."

On the trumpets of the formations they shall write, "The rule of God."

On the trumpets of the men of renown (they shall write), "The heads of the congregation's clans."

Then when they are assembled at the house of meeting, they shall write, "The testimonies of God for a holy congregation."

On the trumpets of the camps they shall write, "The peace of God in the camps of His saints."

On the trumpets for their campaigns they shall write, "The mighty deeds of God to scatter the enemy and to put all those who hate justice to flight and a withdrawal of mercy from all who hate God."

On the trumpets of the battle formations they shall write, "Formations of the divisions of God to avenge His anger on all Sons of Darkness."

On the trumpets for assembling the infantry when the gates of war open that they might go out against the battle line of the enemy, they shall write, "A remembrance of requital at the appointed time of God."

On the trumpets of the slain they shall write, "The hand of the might of God in battle so as to bring down all the slain because of unfaithfulness."

On the trumpets of ambush they shall write, "Mysteries of God to wipe out wickedness."

On the trumpets of pursuit they shall write, "God has struck all of the Sons of Darkness, He shall not diminish His anger until they are annihilated."

When they return from battle to enter the formation, they shall write on the trumpets of retreat, "God has gathered."

On the trumpets for the way of return from battle with the enemy to enter the congregation in Jerusalem, they shall write, "The joy of God in a peaceful return."

Ancient Jews believed Hebrew was the original language spoken by God and Angels and passed down to Adam.

Thus, the language and words have mystical powers. To speak or write Hebrew was to infuse the object spoken to or through with the thoughts and ideas conveyed by the words and bring them into existence just as God spoke and the world came into existence. This would mean when the trumpets were blown, if the banners waved, or weapons deployed, the words and idea written on the instruments would be transmitted to the listener or observer and the messages written on them would become reality. This idea will hold true when statements are written on trumpets and banners and especially when the slogans of war are written upon the weapons such as spears, slings, and swords used against the enemy.

The description of the banners.

 This is the Rule of the Banners of the entire congregation according to their formations. On the grand banner which is at the head of all the people they shall write, "People of God," the names "Israel" and "Aaron," and the names of the twelve tribes of Israel according to their order of birth.

On the banners of the heads of the camps of three tribes they shall write, "the Spirit of God," and the names of three tribes.

On the banner of each tribe they shall write,

"Standard of God," and the name of the leader of the tribe and of its families. (On the banner of the divisions of the ten-thousand write the name of the leader of the ten thousand and the names of the chiefs (of the army) and his hundreds.

On the banner of Merari they shall write, "The Offering of God," and the name of the leader of Merari and the names of the chiefs of his thousands.

According to the Torah, Merari was one of the sons of Levi, and the patriarchal founder of the Merarites, one of the four main divisions among the Levites in Biblical times. The Hebrew word "Merari" means sad or bitter, (from where we also derive the names of Mary and Maria.) The Merarites were charged with the care of the boards of the tabernacle and related items as well as the pillars of the court all around and related components.

Scholars speculate that there were four different groups among the Levites - the Gershonites, Kohathites, Merarites, and Aaronites (or Aaronids). According to some biblical scholars, Levite was originally a job title, deriving from the Minaean word lawi'u meaning priest, rather than having been the name of a tribe. Later the title, being passed down from father to son, became a tribe of its own.

On the banner of the thousand they shall write, "The Anger of God is loosed against Belial and all the men of his forces so that none remain," and the name of the chief of the thousand and the names of the chiefs of his hundreds.

And on the banner of the hundred they shall write, "Hundred of God, the power of war against a sinful flesh," and the name of the chief of the hundred and the names of the chiefs of his tens.

And on the banner of the fifty they shall write, "The might of God have ended the stand of the wicked" and the name of the chief of the fifty and the names of the chiefs of his tens.

On the banner of the thousand they shall write, "The Anger of God is loosed against Belial and all the men of his forces so that none remain."

When they go to battle they shall write on their banners," The truth of God", "The righteousness of God", "The glory of God", "The justice of God", and after these the list of their names in full.

When they draw near for battle they shall write on their banners, "The right hand of God", "The appointed time of God", "The tumult of God", "The slain of God."

After these things, write their names in full. When they return from battle they shall write on their banners, "The exaltation of God," "The greatness of God," "The praise of God," "The glory of God," with their names in full.

The Rule of the banners of the congregation:

When they set out to battle they shall write on the first banner, "The congregation of God," on the second banner write, "The camps of God," on the third write, "The tribes of God," on the fourth write, "The families of God," on the fifth write, "The divisions of God," on the sixth write, "The congregation of God," on the seventh write, "Those called by God," and on the eighth write, "The army of God." They shall write their names in full with all their order. When they come near for battle they shall write on their banners, "The battle of God," "The recompense of God," "The cause of God," "The reprisal of God," "The power of God," "The retribution of God," "The might of God," "The destruction of all the prideful nations by God." And their names in full they shall write upon them.

When they return from battle they shall write on

Joseph Lumpkin

their banners, "The deliverance of God," "The victory of God," "The help of God," "The support of God," "The joy of God," "The thanksgivings of God," "The praise of God," and "The peace of God."

The Length of the Banners.
The banner of the entire congregation shall be fourteen cubits long. The banner of three tribes shall be thirteen cubits long. The banner of a tribe, twelve cubits. The banner of ten thousand, eleven cubits. The banner of a thousand shall be ten cubits. The banner of a hundred shall be nine cubits. The banner of a group of fifty shall be eight cubits, The banner of a group of ten, shall be seven cubits.

The description of the shields.
And on the shield of the Leader of the entire nation they shall write his name, the names "Israel," "Levi," and "Aaron," and the names of the twelve tribes of Israel according to their order of birth, and the names of the twelve chiefs of their tribes.

The description of the arming and deployment of the divisions. This is the rule for arranging the divisions for war when their army is complete to make up the forward battle line:
The battle line shall be formed of one thousand men. There shall be seven forward rows to each

126

battle line, arranged in order. The station of each man will be behind his fellow. All of them shall bear shields of bronze, polished like a face mirror. The shield shall be bound with a border of woven work and a design of loops, the work of a skillful workman consisting of gold, silver, and bronze bound together and jewels in a multicolored brocade. It is the work of a skillful workman, artistically done. The length of the shield shall be two and a half cubits, and its breadth a cubit and a half. In their hands they can hold a lance and a sword.

The length of the lance shall be seven cubits, of which the socket and the blade constitute half a cubit. On the socket there shall be three bands engraved as a border of woven work; of gold, silver, and copper bound together like an artistically designed work. And in the loops of the design, on both sides of the band all around, shall be precious stones, a multicolored brocade, the work of a skillful workman, artistically done, and an ear of grain.

In general, Gold – Purity and redemption, Silver – Wealth, Bronze - Strength. The symbolism of metals representing the Four Kingdoms in Daniel 2 and 3 is expanded in Exodus Rabbah (35:5), "Gold is Babylon;

silver is Media; copper is Greece; iron is Edom (Rome); etc." A symbolic meaning is found by Midrash Tadshe 11 in the fact that of the two altars in the Tabernacle and Temple one was overlaid with gold (the soul) the other with copper (the body).

The socket shall be grooved between the bands like a column, artistically done. The blade shall be of shining white iron, the work of a skillful workman, artistically done, and an ear of grain of pure gold inlaid in the blade. The blade will be tapered towards the point. The swords shall be of refined iron, purified in the furnace and polished like a face mirror, the work of a skillful workman, artistically done, with figures of ears of grain of pure gold embossed on both sides. The borders shall go straight to the point, two on each side. The length of the sword shall be a cubit and a half and its width four fingers. The scabbard shall be four thumbs wide and four handbreadths up to the scabbard. The scabbard shall be tied on either side with thongs of five handbreadths. The handle of the sword shall be of choice horn, the work of a skillful workman, a varicolored design with gold and silver and precious stones. And when the troupes take their stand, they shall arrange seven battle lines, one behind the other and there shall be a space between (the lines) thirty cubits, where the infantry shall stand the (infantry) forward and they shall sling seven times, and return to their position. After them, three divisions of infantry shall advance and stand between the battle lines. The first division shall heave into the enemy battle line seven battle spears.

On the blade of the first spear they shall write, "Flash of a spear for the strength of God."

On the second weapon they shall write, "Missiles of blood to make fall the slain by the wrath of God."

On the third spear they shall write, "The blade of a sword devours the slain of wickedness by the judgment of God." Each of these they shall throw seven times and then return to their position.

After these, two divisions of infantry shall march forth and stand between the two battle lines. The first division will be equipped with a spear and a shield and the second division with a shield and a sword, to bring down the slain by the judgment of God, to subdue the battle line of the enemy by the power of God, and to render recompense for their evil for all the prideful and arrogant nations. So the Kingship shall belong to the God of Israel, and for the holy ones of His people He shall act powerfully.

The description of the deployment of the cavalry.
Seven rows of horsemen shall also take position at the right and at the left of the battle line. Their ranks shall be positioned on both sides, seven hundred horsemen on one side and seven hundred on the other. Two hundred horsemen shall go out with one thousand men of the battle line of the infantry, and they shall take position on all sides of the camp. The total being four thousand six hundred men, and one thousand four hundred cavalry for the entire army arranged for the battle line; fifty for each battle line.

The horsemen with the cavalry of the men of the entire army, will be six thousand made up by five hundred to a tribe. All the cavalry that go out to battle with the infantry shall ride stallions that are swift, responsive, unrelenting, mature, trained for battle, and accustomed to hearing noises and seeing all kinds of scenes.

Those who ride them shall be men capable in battle, trained in horsemanship, the range of their age from thirty to forty-five years. The (head) horsemen of the army shall be from forty to fifty years old, and they shall wear helmets and greaves (shin protectors), carrying in their hands round shields and a lance eight cubits long, and a bow and arrows and battle spears, all of them prepared in (accordance to instructions) to shed the blood of their guilty slain. These are the (instructions of the horsemen.)

The recruitment and age of the soldiers.
The men of the army shall be from forty to fifty years old. The commissioners of the camps shall be from fifty to sixty years old. The officers shall also be from forty to fifty years old. All those who strip the slain, plunder the spoil, cleanse the land, guard the arms, and he who prepares the provisions, all these shall be from twenty-five to thirty years old.

No youth, nor woman shall enter their encampments from the time they leave Jerusalem to go to battle until their return. No one crippled, blind, nor lame, nor a man who has a permanent blemish on his skin, or a man affected with ritual uncleanness of his flesh; none of these shall go with them to battle. All of them shall be volunteers for battle, pure of spirit and flesh, and prepared for the day of vengeance.

Any man who is not ritually clean in respect to his genitals on the day of battle shall not go down with them into battle, for holy angels are present with their army. There shall be a distance between all their camps and the latrine of about two thousand cubits, and no shameful nakedness shall be seen in the areas of all their camps.

The ministry of the priests and Levites.
When the battle line are arrayed against the enemy battle line shall be seven priests that will go through from the middle opening into the gap between the battle lines. The priests will be of the sons of Aaron, dressed in fine white linen garments, consisting of a linen tunic and linen breeches, and girded with a linen sash of twined fine linen of violet, purple, and crimson, and a multicolored colored sign and decorated caps on their heads, , and the garments for battle shall be the work of a skillful workman, and they shall not take them into the sanctuary.

The one priest shall walk before all the men of the battle line to encourage them for battle. In the hands of the remaining six shall be the trumpets of assembly the trumpets of memorial, the trumpets of the alarm, the trumpets of pursuit, and the trumpets of reassembly. When the priests go out into the gap between the battle lines, seven Levites shall go out with them. In their hands shall be seven trumpets of rams' horns. Three officers from among the Levites shall walk before the priests and the Levites. The priests shall blow the two trumpets of assembly.

(And there shall proceed men, with the words of) battle upon fifty shields, and fifty infantrymen shall go out from the one gate and (the) Levites, officers. With each battle line they shall go out according to all (if the) orders given. The men of the infantry (shall go out) from the gates and they shall take position between the two battle lines, and (join) the battle. (Then the priests shall raise the trumpets and) shall blow continually to direct the slingmen until they have completed hurling seven times.

Afterwards the priests shall blow on the trumpets of return, and they shall go along the side of the first battle line to take their position. The priests shall blow on the trumpets of assembly, and the three divisions of infantry shall go out from the gates and stand between the battle lines, and beside them the cavalrymen, at the right and at the left. The priests shall blow on their trumpets a level note, signals for the order of battle. And the columns shall be deployed into their formations, each to his position. When they have positioned themselves in three formations, the priests shall blow for them a second signal, a low legato note, signals for advance, until they come near the battle line of the enemy and take hold of their weapons. Then the priests shall blow on the six trumpets of the slain a sharp staccato note to direct the battle, and the Levites and all the people with rams' horns shall blow a great battle alarm together in order to melt the heart of the enemy.

With the sound of the alarm, the battle spears shall fly out to bring down the slain. Then the sound of the rams' horns shall quiet, but on the trumpets the priests shall continue to blow a sharp staccato note to direct the signals of battle until they have hurled into the battle line of the enemy seven times. Afterwards, the priests shall blow for them the trumpets of retreat, a low note, level and legato (smooth). According to this rule the priests shall blow for the three divisions. When the first division throws, the priests and the Levites and all the people with rams' horns shall blow a great alarm to direct the battle until they have hurled seven times.

Afterwards, the priests shall on the trumpets of retreat blow for them. And they shall take their stand in their positions in the battle line and shall take up position (in front of the) slain, and all the people with rams' horns shall blow a very loud battle alarm, and as the sound goes out their hands shall begin to bring down the slain, and all the people shall quiet the sound of alarm, but the priests shall continue sounding on the trumpets of the slain to direct the fighting, until the enemy is defeated and turns in retreat.

The shofar (ram's horn) is often used as an instrument of spiritual warfare. the Torah states, "When you go to war in your land against an adversary who is oppressing you, you are to sound an alarm with trumpets; then you will be remembered before the LORD your God and you will be saved from your enemies." Num. 10:9 It is sounded during Shavuot and the high holy days.

The priests shall blow the alarm to direct the battle, and when they have been defeated before them, the priests shall blow the trumpets of assembly, and all the infantry shall go out to them from the midst of the front battle lines and stand, six divisions in addition to the division which is engaged in battle: altogether, seven battle lines, twenty-eight thousand soldiers, and six thousand horsemen. All these shall pursue in order to destroy the enemy in God's battle; a total annihilation.

The priests shall blow for them the trumpets of pursuit, and they shall divide themselves for a pursuit of annihilation against all the enemy. The cavalry shall push the enemy back at the flanks of the battle until they are destroyed. When the slain have fallen, the priests shall continue blowing from afar and shall not enter into the midst of the slain so as to be defiled by their unclean blood, for they are holy. They shall not allow the oil of their priestly anointment to be profaned with the blood of the vainglorious nations.

We continually see the alternating and interposed numbers of six and seven. Trumpets sound 6 times. Weapons are deployed seven times in a row by a soldier before the next soldier steps up and deploys seven more times. Six times the trumpets are blown by the priests. The priests represent the highest spiritual level of man, which always falls short and needs God. This is the meaning of six. Seven represents the power and perfection of God, who is guiding the weapons. Both weapons and trumpets and inscribed with the words of faith and action, given to the people by God.

The description of the maneuvers of the battle divisions.

This is the Rule for changing the order of the battle divisions, in order to arrange their position against (the enemy in) a pincer movement and towers, line, arc, and towers, and as it draws slowly forward, then the columns and the flanks go out from the two sides of the battle line that the enemy might become discouraged. The shields of the soldiers of the towers shall be three cubits long, and their lances eight cubits long. The towers shall go out from the battle line with one hundred shields on a side. They shall surround the tower on the three front-most sides, three hundred shields in all. There shall be three gates to a tower, one on the right and one on the left. Upon all the shields of the tower soldiers they shall write: on the first, "Michael" and on the second, "Gabriel," on the third, "Seriel," and on the fourth "Raphael." "Michael" and "Gabriel" on the right, and "Raphael" and "Seriel" on the left. And (push the enemy) to the four(th) (side). They shall establish an ambush for the battle line of (three sides) and they shall fall on the slain.

Michael - *is a male given name that comes from the Hebrew "Who is like God" (literally, "Who is like El). Michael is mentioned three times in the Book of Daniel, once as a "great prince who stands up for the children of your people". The idea that Michael was the advocate of the Jews became so prevalent a rabbinical prohibition was issued against appealing to angels as intermediaries between God and his people, Michael came to occupy a certain place in the Jewish liturgy as the general over God's army.*

Gabriel - *God is my strength. Gabriel is an archangel who, according to several religions, typically serves as a messenger sent from God to certain people. He appeared to the prophet Daniel, delivering explanations of Daniel's visions (Daniel 8:15–26, 9:21–27). In the Gospel of Luke, Gabriel appeared to Zecharias, and to the virgin Mary, foretelling the births of John the Baptist and Jesus, respectively (Luke 1:11–38). He is mentioned in the Intertestamental period sources such as the Book of Enoch. Roman Catholic, Anglican, Lutheran, Eastern and Oriental Orthodox churches reference the archangels Michael, Raphael, and Gabriel.*

Raphael - *"It is God who heals". Raphael is the fourth major angel. In Muslim tradition he is known as Israfil. Raphael is mentioned in the Book of Tobit, which is accepted as canonical by Catholics, Orthodox, and some Anglo-Catholics churches. The book is considered useful for public teaching by Lutherans and Anglicans. Raphael is generally associated with the angel mentioned in the Gospel of John as stirring the water at the healing pool of Bethesda.*

Seriel - *"Command of God" "God's command") (alternate translation – "Minister of God") is one of the archangels mainly from Judaic tradition. Other possible* *versions of his name are Suriel, Suriyel (in some Dead Sea Scrolls translations), Sauriel, Surya, Saraqael, Sarakiel, Suruel, Surufel and Sourial. Suriel is a prince of presence and like Raphael, an angel of healing. He is also a benevolent angel of death (one of a few). Suriel was sent to retrieve the soul of Moses.*

The address of the chief priest.

(…) of our camps, and to keep ourselves from any shameful nakedness, and he (Moses) told us that You are in our midst, (and You are) a great and awesome God, plundering all of our enemies before us. He taught us from (the times) of old through out generations, saying, when you approach the battle, the priest shall stand and speak unto the people, saying, 'Hear O Israel, you are approaching the battle against your enemies today. Do not be afraid nor fainthearted. Do not tremble, nor be terrified because of them, for your God goes with you, to fight for you against your enemies, and to save you"'

Deuteronomy 20 New International Version (NIV)
Going to War
20 When you go to war against your enemies and see horses and chariots and an army greater than yours, do not be afraid of them, because the Lord your God, who brought you up out of Egypt, will be with you. 2 When

you are about to go into battle, the priest shall come forward and address the army. 3 He shall say: "Hear, Israel: Today you are going into battle against your enemies. Do not be fainthearted or afraid; do not panic or be terrified by them. 4 For the Lord your God is the one who goes with you to fight for you against your enemies to give you victory."

Our officers shall speak to all those prepared for battle, those of willing heart, to strengthen them by the might of God, to turn back all who have lost heart, and to strengthen all the valiant warriors together. They shall recount that which You have spoken by the hand of Moses, saying: "And when there is a war in your land against the adversary who attacks you, then you shall sound an alarm with the trumpets that you might be remembered before your God and be saved from your enemies

Numbers 10 NIV
The Silver Trumpets
10 The Lord said to Moses: 2 "Make two trumpets of hammered silver, and use them for calling the community together and for having the camps set out. 3 When both are sounded, the whole community is to assemble before you at the entrance to the tent of meeting. 4 If only one is sounded, the leaders – the heads of the clans of Israel – are to assemble before you. 5

When a trumpet blast is sounded, the tribes camping on the east are to set out. 6 At the sounding of a second blast, the camps on the south are to set out. The blast will be the signal for setting out. 7 To gather the assembly, blow the trumpets, but not with the signal for setting out.

8 "The sons of Aaron, the priests, are to blow the trumpets. This is to be a lasting ordinance for you and the generations to come. 9 When you go into battle in your own land against an enemy who is oppressing you, sound a blast on the trumpets. Then you will be remembered by the Lord your God and rescued from your enemies. 10 Also at your times of rejoicing – your appointed festivals and New Moon feasts – you are to sound the trumpets over your burnt offerings and fellowship offerings, and they will be a memorial for you before your God. I am the Lord your God."

The prayer of the chief priest.

Who is like You, O God of Israel, in heaven and on earth, that he can perform like you do with Your great works and Your great strength? Who is like Your people Israel, whom You have chosen for Yourself from all the peoples of the lands? They are people sanctified by the covenant, learned in the statutes, enlightened in understanding. Those who hear the glorious voice and see the holy angels, whose ears are open to hearing deep things. O God,

You have created the expanse of the skies, the host of the stars (luminaries), the work of spirits and the dominion of holy ones, the treasures of Your glory in the clouds.

Rev. 21: 7 He who overcomes will inherit all this, and I will be his God and he will be my son. 8 But the cowardly, the unbelieving, the vile, the murderers, the sexually immoral, those who practice magic arts, the idolaters and all liars – their place will be in the fiery lake of burning sulfur. This is the second death."

8 But with the righteous He will make peace; and will protect the elect and mercy shall be on them. And they shall all belong to God, and they shall prosper, and they shall be blessed. And the light of God shall shine on them. 9 And behold! He comes with ten thousand of His holy ones (saints) to execute judgment on all, and to destroy all the ungodly (wicked); and to convict all flesh of all the works of their ungodliness which they have ungodly committed, and of all the hard things which ungodly sinners have spoken against Him.

Rev. 21: 23 The city does not need the sun or the moon to shine on it, for the glory of God gives it light, and the Lamb is its lamp. 24 The nations will walk by its light, and the kings of the earth will bring their splendor into it. 25 On no day will its gates ever be shut, for there will be no night there.

JUD 1:14   And Enoch also, the seventh from Adam, prophesied of these, saying, Behold, the Lord cometh with ten thousands of his saints, 15   To execute judgment upon all, and to convince all that are ungodly among them of all their ungodly deeds which they have ungodly committed, and of all their hard speeches which ungodly sinners have spoken against him.

He who created the earth and the limits of her divisions into wilderness and plains, and autumn, winter, and spring with its fruits; the circle of the seas, the sources of the rivers, and the rift of the deeps, wild beasts and winged creatures, the form of man and the generations of his seed, the confusion of language and the separation of peoples, the abode of families which have the inheritance of the lands, and holy festivals, courses of years and times of eternity.

Book of Enoch [Chapter 2]
1 Observe everything that takes place in the sky, how the lights do not change their orbits, and the luminaries which are in heaven, how they all rise and set in order each in its season (proper time), and do not transgress (defy) their appointed order.
2 Consider the earth, and understand the things which

143

take place on it from start to finish, how steadfast they are, how none of the things on the earth change, but all the works of God appear to you.

3 Behold the summer and the winter, how the whole earth is filled with water, and clouds and dew and rain lie on it.

[Chapter 3]

1 Observe and see how (in the winter) all the trees seem as though they had withered and shed all their leaves, except fourteen trees, which do not lose their foliage but retain the old foliage from two to three years until the new comes.

[Chapter 4]

1 And again, observe the days of summer how the sun is above the earth. And you seek shade and shelter because of the heat of the sun, and the earth also burns with growing heat, and so you cannot walk on the earth, or on a rock because of its heat.

[Chapter 5]

1 Observe how the trees are covered with green leaves and how they bear fruit. Understand, know, and

recognize that He that lives for ever made them this way
for you.

2 And all His works go on before Him from year to year
for ever, and all the work and the tasks which they
accomplish for Him do not change, and so is it done.

3 Consider how the sea and the rivers in like manner
accomplish their course do not change because of His
commandments.

4 But you, you have neither held to nor have you done
the commandments of the Lord, But you have turned
away and spoken proud and hard words with your
unclean mouths against His greatness. Oh, you hard-
hearted, you shall find no peace.

5 Therefore shall you curse your days, and the years of
your life shall perish, and the years of your destruction
shall be multiplied and in an eternal curse you shall find
no mercy.

6 In those days you shall make your names an eternal
curse to all the righteous, and by you shall all who curse,
curse, and all the sinners and godless shall curse you
forever. And for you the godless there shall be a curse.

7 And all the elect shall rejoice, and there shall be
forgiveness of sins, and mercy and peace and forbearance
and joy. There shall be salvation for them, (like/and) a
good light. And for all of you sinners there shall be no
salvation, but on you all shall abide a curse.

8 But for the elect there shall be light and joy and peace,

and they shall inherit the earth.

9 And then wisdom shall be given to the elect, and they shall all live and never again sin, either through forgetfulness or through pride: But those who are given wisdom shall be humble.

10 And they shall not again transgress, Nor shall they sin all the days of their life, Nor shall they die of the anger or wrath of God, But they shall complete the number of the days of their lives. And their lives shall be increased in peace, and their years will grow in joy and eternal gladness and peace, all the days of their lives.

(Deuteronomy 11: 26 See, I am setting before you today a blessing and a curse- 27 the blessing if you obey the commands of the LORD your God that I am giving you today; 28 the curse if you disobey the commands of the LORD your God and turn from the way that I command you today by following other gods, which you have not known.)

(Isaiah 65

1 I am sought of them that asked not for me; I am found of them that sought me not: I said, Behold me, behold me, unto a nation that was not called by my name.

2 I have spread out my hands all the day unto a rebellious people, which walketh in a way that was not good, after their own thoughts;

3 A people that provoketh me to anger continually to my face; that sacrificeth in gardens, and burneth incense upon altars of brick;

4 Which remain among the graves, and lodge in the monuments, which eat swine's flesh, and broth of abominable things is in their vessels;

5 Which say, Stand by thyself, come not near to me; for I am holier than thou. These are a smoke in my nose, a fire that burneth all the day.

6 Behold, it is written before me: I will not keep silence, but will recompense, even recompense into their bosom,

7 Your iniquities, and the iniquities of your fathers together, saith the LORD, which have burned incense upon the mountains, and blasphemed me upon the hills: therefore will I measure their former work into their bosom.

8 Thus saith the LORD, As the new wine is found in the cluster, and one saith, Destroy it not; for a blessing is in it: so will I do for my servants' sakes, that I may not destroy them all.

9 And I will bring forth a seed out of Jacob, and out of Judah an inheritor of my mountains: and mine elect shall inherit it, and my servants shall dwell there.)

(Only) these we know from Your understanding which (You have taught us.) And Your ears (listen) to our cry, for (the protection of) this house. Truly the battle is Yours, and by the strength of Your hand their corpses have been broken to pieces, without anyone to bury them. Indeed, Goliath the Gittite, a mighty man of valor, You delivered into the hand of David, Your servant, because he trusted in Your great name and not in sword and spear. For the battle is Yours. He subdued the Philistines many times by Your holy name. Also by the hand of our kings You rescued us many times because of Your mercy; not according to our works, for we have acted wickedly, nor for the acts of our rebelliousness. The battle is Yours, the strength is from You, it is not our own. Neither our power nor the strength of our hand have done valiantly, but rather by Your power and the strength of Your great valor.

Just as You told us in time past, saying: "There shall come forth a star out of Jacob, a scepter shall rise out of Israel, and shall crush the forehead of Moab and tear down all sons of Sheth (the noisy boasters), and he shall descend on Jacob and shall destroy the remnant from the city, and the enemy shall be a possession, and Israel shall do valiantly

Numbers 24 New International Version (NIV)
1 Now when Balaam saw that it pleased the Lord to bless Israel, he did not resort to divination as at other times,

but turned his face toward the wilderness.
2 When Balaam looked out and saw Israel encamped
tribe by tribe, the Spirit of God came on him
3 and he spoke his message:

"The prophecy of Balaam son of Beor,
  the prophecy of one whose eye sees clearly,
4 the prophecy of one who hears the words of God,
  who sees a vision from the Almighty,[a]
  who falls prostrate, and whose eyes are opened:
5 How beautiful are your tents, Jacob,
  your dwelling places, Israel!
6 Like valleys they spread out,
  like gardens beside a river,
like aloes planted by the Lord,
  like cedars beside the waters.
7 Water will flow from their buckets;
  their seed will have abundant water.
Their king will be greater than Agag;
  their kingdom will be exalted.
8 God brought them out of Egypt;
  they have the strength of a wild ox.
They devour hostile nations
  and break their bones in pieces;
  with their arrows they pierce them.
9 Like a lion they crouch and lie down,
  like a lioness – who dares to rouse them?
 May those who bless you be blessed

and those who curse you be cursed!"

10 Then Balak's anger burned against Balaam. He struck his hands together and said to him, "I summoned you to curse my enemies, but you have blessed them these three times. 11 Now leave at once and go home! I said I would reward you handsomely, but the Lord has kept you from being rewarded."

12 Balaam answered Balak, "Did I not tell the messengers you sent me,

13 'Even if Balak gave me all the silver and gold in his palace, I could not do anything of my own accord, good or bad, to go beyond the command of the Lord – and I must say only what the Lord says'?

14 Now I am going back to my people, but come, let me warn you of what this people will do to your people in days to come."

Balaam's Fourth Message
15 Then he spoke his message:
The prophecy of Balaam son of Beor,
  the prophecy of one whose eye sees clearly,
16 the prophecy of one who hears the words of God,
  who has knowledge from the Most High,
who sees a vision from the Almighty,
  who falls prostrate, and whose eyes are opened:
17 I see him, but not now;
  I behold him, but not near.
A star will come out of Jacob;

a scepter will rise out of Israel.
He will crush the foreheads of Moab,
the skulls[b] of[c] all the people of Sheth.[d]
18 *Edom will be conquered;*
Seir, his enemy, will be conquered,
but Israel will grow strong.
19 *A ruler will come out of Jacob*
and destroy the survivors of the city.

Balaam's Fifth Message
20 *Then Balaam saw Amalek and spoke his message:*
"Amalek was first among the nations,
but their end will be utter destruction."

Balaam's Sixth Message
21 *Then he saw the Kenites and spoke his message:*
"Your dwelling place is secure,
your nest is set in a rock;
22 *yet you Kenites will be destroyed*
when Ashur takes you captive."

Balaam's Seventh Message
23 *Then he spoke his message:*
"Alas! Who can live when God does this?[e]
24   *Ships will come from the shores of Cyprus;*
they will subdue Ashur and Eber,
but they too will come to ruin."
25 *Then Balaam got up and returned home, and Balak*

went his own way.

Footnotes:
  Numbers 24:4 Hebrew Shaddai; also in verse 16
  Numbers 24:17 Samaritan Pentateuch (see also Jer. 48:45); the meaning of the word in the Masoretic Text is uncertain.
  Numbers 24:17 Or possibly Moab, / batter
  Numbers 24:17 Or all the noisy boasters
  Numbers 24:23 Masoretic Text; with a different word division of the Hebrew The people from the islands will gather from the north.

By the hand of Your anointed ones, seers of things appointed, You have told us about the times of the wars of Your hands in order that You may glorify Yourself (and fight) among our enemies to bring down the hordes of Belial, the seven nations of empty, boasting, prideful nations, at the hand of the oppressed whom You have redeemed with power and retribution; and wondrous strength.

A heart that melts shall be as a door of hope. You will do to them as You did to Pharaoh and the officers of his chariots in the Red Sea. You will ignite the humble of spirit like a fiery torch of fire in a sheaf, consuming the wicked.

You shall not turn back until the annihilation of the guilty. In time past You foretold the appointed time for Your hand is powerful work against the Kittim, saying: And Assyria shall fall by a sword not of man, and a sword, 'not of men, shall consume him.

Isaiah 31 New International Version (NIV)
Woe to Those Who Rely on Egypt

31 Woe to those who go down to Egypt for help,
    who rely on horses,
who trust in the multitude of their chariots
    and in the great strength of their horsemen,
but do not look to the Holy One of Israel,
    or seek help from the Lord.
2 Yet he too is wise and can bring disaster;
    he does not take back his words.
He will rise up against that wicked nation,
    against those who help evildoers.
3 But the Egyptians are mere mortals and not God;
    their horses are flesh and not spirit.
When the Lord stretches out his hand,
    those who help will stumble,
    those who are helped will fall;
    all will perish together.
4 This is what the Lord says to me:

"As a lion growls,

a great lion over its prey —
and though a whole band of shepherds
   is called together against it,
it is not frightened by their shouts
   or disturbed by their clamor —
so the Lord Almighty will come down
   to do battle on Mount Zion and on its heights.
5 Like birds hovering overhead,
   the Lord Almighty will shield Jerusalem;
he will shield it and deliver it,
   he will 'pass over' it and will rescue it."
6 Return, you Israelites, to the One you have so greatly
revolted against. 7 For in that day every one of you will
reject the idols of silver and gold your sinful hands have
made.
8 "Assyria will fall by no human sword;
   a sword, not of mortals, will devour them.
They will flee before the sword
   and their young men will be put to forced labor.
9 Their stronghold will fall because of terror;
   at the sight of the battle standard their commanders
will panic,"
declares the Lord,
   whose fire is in Zion,
   whose furnace is in Jerusalem.

For into the hand of the oppressed You will deliver

the enemies of all the lands; into the hands of those who are prostrate in the dust, in order to bring down all mighty men of (faithless) peoples, to return the recompense of the wicked on the head of (the guilty) to pronounce the fair judgment of Your truth on all sons of man, and to make for Yourself an everlasting name among the people.

(Give us victory in) wars, and to show Yourself great and holy before the remnant of the nations, so that they may know that You are God when You carry out judgments on (Gog and on all his company that are assembled all around us. For You will do battle against them from the heavens (and heap) upon them for confusion. For You have a multitude of holy ones in the heavens and hosts of angels in Your exalted dwelling to praise Your name.

The chosen ones of the holy people You have established for Yourself in a community. The number and The book of the names of all their host is with You in Your holy dwelling, and the number of the holy ones is in the abode of Your glory. Mercies of blessing (is with them) and Your covenant of peace You engraved for them with a stylus of life in order to reign over them for all time, commissioning the hosts of Your elect by their thousands and tens of thousands together with Your holy ones and Your angels, and directing them in battle so as to condemn the earthly adversaries by trial with Your judgments. With the elect of heaven they shall prevail.

And You, O God, are awesome in the glory of Your dominion, and the company of Your holy ones is in our midst for eternal support. We shall direct our contempt at kings, derision and disdain at mighty men. For the Lord is holy, and the King of Glory is with us together with the holy ones. Mighty men and a host of angels are with our commissioned forces. The Hero of War is with our company, and the host of His spirits is with our steps. Our horse riders are as the clouds and as the mist covering the earth, and as a steady downpour shedding judgment on all her offspring.

Rise up, O Hero, take Your captives, O Glorious One, take Your plunder, O You who do valiantly. Lay Your hand upon the neck of Your enemies, and Your foot upon the backs of the slain. Crush the nations, Your adversaries, and may Your sword devour guilty flesh. Fill Your land with glory, and Your heritage with blessing.

Book of Enoch

The Book of Watchers (Chapters 1-36):
[Chapter 1]

1 The words of the blessing of Enoch, with which he blessed the elect and righteous, who will be living in the day of tribulation, when all the wicked and godless people are to be removed (from the earth).

2 And he began his story saying: (I am) Enoch, a righteous man, whose eyes were opened by God, and who saw the vision of the Holy One in heaven, which the angels showed me. And I heard everything from them, and I saw and understood, but it was not for this generation (to know), but for a remote one which is to come.

3 As I began my story concerning the elect I said,: The Holy Great One will come out from His dwelling,

4 And the eternal God will tread on the earth, (even) on Mount Sinai, and appear in the strength of His might from heaven.

5 And all shall be very afraid. The Watchers shall shake, and great fear and trembling shall seize them all the way to the ends of the earth.

6 And the high mountains shall be shaken, and the high hills shall be laid low, and shall melt like wax in the flame.

7 And the earth shall be completely torn apart, and all that is on the earth shall be destroyed, And there shall be a judgment on all.

An abundance of cattle in Your fields; silver and gold, and precious stones in Your palaces. O Zion, rejoice greatly, and shine with joyful songs, O Jerusalem. Rejoice, all you cities of Judah, open your gates forever that the wealth of the nations might be brought to you, and their kings shall serve you.

David was king and his praise was to ring out and shine:
All they that oppressed you shall bow down to you, and the dust of your feet they shall lick. O daughters of my people shout out with a voice of joy, adorn yourselves with ornaments of glory Rule over the kingdom, and Israel to reign eternally.(…) them the mighty men of war, O Jerusalem be exalted above the heavens, O Lord, and let Your glory be above all the earth.

The blessings of the war recited by all the leaders after the victory.
And then the Chief Priest shall stand and his brothers the priests, the Levites, and all the elders of the Army with him. They shall bless from their position, the God of Israel and all His works of

truth, and they shall curse Belial there and all the spirits of his forces.

And they shall say response: "Blessed is the God of Israel for all His holy purpose and His works of truth. And blessed are those who serve Him righteously. who know Him by faith. And cursed is Belial for his contentious purpose, and accursed for his reprehensible rule. And cursed are all the spirits of his lot for their wicked purpose. Accursed are they for all their filthy dirty service. For they are the lot of darkness, but the lot of God is light eternal. You are the God of our fathers. We bless Your name forever, for we are an eternal people. You made a covenant with our fathers, and will establish it for their seed throughout the ages of eternity. In all the testimonies of Your glory there has been remembrance of Your kindness in our midst as an assistance to the remnant and the survivors for the sake of Your covenant and to recount Your works of truth and the judgments of Your wondrous strength.

And You, O God, created us for Yourself as an eternal people, and into the lot of light You cast us in accordance with Your truth. You appointed the Prince of Light from of old to assist us, for in His lot are all sons of righteousness and all spirits of truth are in his dominion.

You yourself made Belial for the pit, an angel of malevolence, his dominion is in darkness and his counsel is to condemn and convict. All the spirits of his lot are the angels of destruction who walk in accord with the rule of darkness, for it is their only desire. But we, in the lot of Your truth, rejoice in Your mighty hand. We rejoice in Your salvation, and revel in Your help and Your peace. Who is like You in strength, O God of Israel, and yet Your mighty hand is with the oppressed. What angel or prince is like You for Your effectual support, for of old You appointed for Yourself a day of great battle to support truth and to destroy iniquity, to bring darkness low and to lend might to light, and for an eternal stand, and to annihilate all the Sons of Darkness and bring joy to all the Sons of Light for You Yourself designated us for an appointed time like the fire of His fury against the idols of Egypt.

The blessings of the war recited by all the leaders in the morning before the battle. After they have withdrawn from the slain to enter the camp, all of them shall sing the hymn of return. In the morning they shall wash their clothes, cleanse themselves of the blood of the sinful bodies, and return to the place where they had stood, where they had formed the battle line before the slain of the enemy fell.

There they shall all bless the God of Israel and together they shall joyously exalt His name. They shall say in response: "Blessed is the God of Israel, who guards loving-kindness for His covenant and the appointed times of salvation for the people He redeems.

He has called those who stumble unto wondrous accomplishments, and
He has gathered a congregation of nations for annihilation without remnant in order to raise up in judgment he whose heart has melted, to open a mouth for the dumb to sing God's mighty deeds, and to teach feeble hands warfare. He gives those whose knees shake strength to stand, and strengthens those who have been beaten from the hips to the shoulder.

Among the poor in spirit (there is not) a hard heart, and by those whose way is perfect shall all wicked nations come to an end. There will be no place for all their mighty men. But we are the remnant of Your people. Blessed is Your name, O God of loving-kindness, the One who kept the covenant for our forefathers. Throughout all our generations

You have made Your mercies wondrous for the remnant of the people during the dominion of Belial. With all the mysteries of his hatred they have not led us astray from Your covenant. His spirits of destruction You have driven away from us. And when the men of his dominion condemned themselves, You have preserved the lives of Your redeemed. You raised up the small fallen by Your strength, but those who are great in height You will cut down to humble them. And there is no rescuer for all their mighty men, and no place of refuge for their swift ones. To their honored men You will return shame, and all their vain existence shall be as nothing.

But we, Your holy people, shall praise Your name for Your works of truth. Because of Your mighty deeds we shall exalt your splendor in epochs and appointed times of eternity, at the beginning of day, at night and at dawn and dusk. For Your glorious purpose is great and Your wondrous mysteries are in Your high heavens, to raise up those for Yourself from the dust and to humble those of the gods.

Rise up, rise up, O God of gods, and raise Yourself in power, O King of Kings (and) let all the Sons of Darkness scatter from before You. Let the light of

Your majesty shine forever upon gods and men, as a fire burning in the dark places of the damned. Let it burn the damned of Sheol, (who are) eternal burning among the transgressors (throughout) all the appointed times of eternity."

Comments such as "God of Israel, King of Kings, and God of gods," shows a belief in polytheism or an acceptance that there were other gods worshipped by other peoples. These gods were viewed as lesser but apparently still acknowledged as gods.

They shall repeat all the thanksgiving hymns of battle there and then return to their camps. For it is a time of distress for Israel, a fixed time of battle against all the nations. The purpose of God is eternal redemption, and annihilation for all nations of wickedness. All those prepared for battle shall set out and camp opposite the king of the Kittim and all the forces of Belial that are assembled with him for a day of vengeance by the sword of God. The final battle the first engagement.

Then the Chief Priest shall stand, and with him his brothers the priests, the Levites, and all the men of the army. He shall read aloud the prayer for the appointed time of battle, as is written in the book "The Rule of His Time", including all the words of their thanksgivings. Then he shall form there all the battle lines, as written in "The Book of the War."

Then the priest appointed for the time of vengeance by all his brothers shall walk about and encourage them for the battle, and he shall say in response: "Be strong and courageous as warriors. Fear not, nor be discouraged and let not your heart be faint.

Do not panic, neither be alarmed because of them. Do not turn back nor flee from them. For they are a wicked congregation, all their deeds are in darkness; it is their desire. They have established all their refuge in a lie, their strength is as smoke that vanishes, and all their vast assembly is as chaff which blows away (and they will become a) desolation, and shall not be found.

Every creature of greed shall wither quickly away like a flower at harvest time. Come, strengthen yourselves for the battle of God, for this day is an appointed time of battle for God against all the nations and bring judgment upon all flesh. The God of Israel is raising His hand in His wondrous strength against all the spirits of wickedness and the mighty ones of the gods are girding themselves for battle, and the formations of the holy ones are readying themselves for a day of vengeance against the God of Israel (but He will hasten) to remove

Belial in his hell until every source of (him) is come to an end. For the God of Israel has called out a sword against all the nations, and by the holy ones of His people He will do mightily."

They shall carry out all the Rule on that day at the place where they stand opposite the camps of the Kittim. Then the priests shall blow for them the trumpets of remembrance. The gates of war shall open, and the infantry shall go out and stand in columns between the battle lines. (and stand in the gap.)

Ezekiel 22:30 New International Version
"I looked for someone among them who would build up the wall and stand before me in the gap on behalf of the land so I would not have to destroy it, but I found no one

The priests shall blow for them a signal for the formation and the columns shall deploy at the sound of the trumpets until each man has taken his station.

Then the priests shall blow for them a second signal, (which is the signal) for confrontation. When they stand near the battle line of the Kittim, within throwing range, each man shall raise his hand with his weapon of war.

Then the six priests shall blow on the trumpets of the slain a sharp staccato note to direct the fighting. The Levites and the all the people with rams' horns shall blow a battle signal, a loud noise. As the sound goes forth, the infantry shall begin to bring down the slain of the Kittim, and all the people shall cease the signal, but the priests shall continue blowing on the trumpets of the slain and the battle shall prevail against the Kittim.

The final battle the second engagement.
When Belial prepares himself to assist the Sons of Darkness, and the slain among the infantry begin to fall by God's mysteries, to test by these mysteries and all those appointed for battle, the priests shall blow the trumpets of assembly so that another battle line might go forth as a battle reserve, and they shall take up position between the battle lines.

For those employed in battle they shall blow a signal to return. Then the Chief Priest shall approach and stand before the battle line, and shall encourage their heart by the wondrous might of God and fortify their hands for His battle. And he shall say in response: "Blessed is God, for He tests the heart of His people in the crucible. And (do) not (worry about) your slain. For you have obeyed, from of old, the mysteries of God.

Now as for you, take courage and stand in the gap, do not fear when God strengthens (you, for in the) land He shall appoint their retribution with burning (for) those tested by the crucible. He shall sharpen the implements of war, and they shall not become blunt until all the nations off wickedness come to an end.

But, as for you, remember the judgment of Nadab and Abihu, the sons of Aaron, by whose judgment God showed Himself holy before all the people.
But Eleazar and Ithamar He preserved for Himself for an eternal covenant of priesthood. But, as for you, take courage and do not fear them, for their end is emptiness and their desire is for the void. Their support is without strength and they do not know that from the God of Israel is all that is and that will be. He (alone is) in all which exists for eternity. Today is His appointed time to subdue and to humiliate the prince of the realms of wickedness. He will send eternal support to the company of His redeemed by the power of the majestic angel of the authority of Michael. By eternal light He shall joyfully light up the covenant of Israel peace and blessing for the lot of God to exalt the authority of Michael among the gods and

the dominion of Israel among all flesh. Righteousness shall rejoice on high, and all sons of His truth shall rejoice in eternal knowledge. But as for you, O sons of His covenant, take courage in God's crucible, until He shall wave His hand and complete His fiery trials; His mysteries concerning your existence."

In the Book of Exodus, the Book of Leviticus and the Book of Numbers, Nadab and Abihu were respectively the eldest and second-eldest of the sons of Aaron. They offered a sacrifice with strange fire before the LORD, disobeying his instructions. they were consumed immediately by God's fire. The priests were commanded not to mourn, but the people at large were permitted.

The final battle the third engagement.

And after these words, the priests shall blow for them a signal to form the divisions of the battle line. The columns shall be deployed at the sound of the trumpets, until each man has taken his station. Then the priests shall blow another signal on the trumpets, that the signal for confrontation. When the infantry has approached the battle line of the Kittim, within throwing range, each man shall raise his hand with his weapon.

Then the priests shall blow on the trumpets of the

slain and the Levites and all the people with ram's horns shall sound a signal for battle. The infantry shall attack the army of the Kittim, and as the sound of the signal goes forth, they shall begin to bring down their slain. Then all the people shall cease the sound of the signal, while the priests continuously blow on the trumpets of the slain, and the battle prevails against the Kittim, and the troops of Belial are defeated before them. Thus in the third lot (the army are destined to fall slain.)

Author's note: The sections of the final battle involving the fourth, fifth, and sixth engagements are not legible. The codex has large pieces missing. Nothing of these engagements is preserved.

The final battle the seventh engagement.
… And in the seventh lot, the great hand of God shall be lifted up against Belial and against all the forces of his dominion for an eternal slaughter. The shout of the holy ones (will go forth) when they pursue Assyria. Then the sons of Japheth shall fall, never to rise again, and the Kitum shall be crushed without remnant or survivor. So the God of Israel shall raise His hand against the entire multitude of Belial. At that time the priests shall sound a signal on the six trumpets of remembrance, and all the battle formations shall be gathered to them and

divide against all the camps of the Kittim to completely destroy them. And when the sun hastens to set on that day, the Chief Priest and the priests and the Levites who are with him, and the chiefs of the battle lines and the men of the army shall bless the God of Israel there. They shall say in response: Blessed is Your name, O God of gods, for You have done wondrous things for Your people, and have kept Your covenant for us from of old. Many times You have opened the gates of salvation for us for the sake of Your covenant. And You provided for our affliction in accord with Your goodness toward us. You, O God of righteousness, have acted for the sake of Your name.

Thanksgiving for final victory.

. . . You have done wonders upon wonders with us, but from (times) of old there has been nothing like it, for You have known our appointed time. Today Your power has shined forth for us, and You have shown us the hand of Your mercies with us in eternal redemption, in order to remove the dominion of the enemy, that it might be no more. (This is) the hand of Your strength. In battle, You shall show Yourself strong against our enemies for an absolute slaughter. Now the day is pressing upon us to pursue their multitude, for You (go before us) and the heart of warriors You have broken so that no one is able to stand. Yours is the might, and the battle is in Your hand, and there is no God like You. Your (. . .) and the appointed times of Your will, and reprisal (...) Your enemies, and You will cut off from (...) .

And we shall direct our contempt at kings, (and our) derision and disdain at mighty men. For our Majestic One is holy. The King of Glory is with us and the host of His spirits is with our steps. Our horsemen are as the clouds and as the mist covering the earth; as a steady downpour shedding judgment on all her offspring.

Rise up, O Hero, Take Your captives, O Glorious One, and take Your plunder, O You Who do valiantly. Lay Your hand upon the neck of Your enemies, and Your foot upon the backs of the slain. Crush the nations, and Your adversaries, and let Your sword devour flesh. Fill Your land with glory, and Your inheritance with blessing. An abundance of cattle is in Your fields, silver and gold in Your palaces. O Zion, rejoice greatly, and rejoice, all you cities of Judah. Open your gates forever, so that the wealth of the nations might be brought to you, and their kings shall serve you. All they that oppressed you shall bow down to you, and they shall lick the dust of your feet. O daughters of my people, burst out with a voice of joy. Adorn yourselves with ornaments of glory, and rule over the kingdom of the (Kittim). Your (...) and Israel for an eternal dominion.

Ceremony after the final battle.
Then they shall gather in the camp that night for rest until the morning. In the morning they shall come to the place of the battle line, where the mighty men of the Kittim fell, as well as the multitude of Assyria, and the forces of all the nations that were assembled unto them, to see whether the multitude of slain are dead with none to bury them; those who fell there by the sword of God.

And the High Priest shall approach there with his deputy, his brothers the priests, and the Levites with the Leader of the battle, and all the chiefs of the battle lines and their officers (and they shall come) together. When they stand before the slain of the Kittim, they shall praise there the God of Israel. And they shall say in response (Glory to) God most high...

TheWar Scroll

Conclusion

For thousands of years Israel has awaited the judgment and redemption of The Lord. When the world seemed the most unfair and brutal, hope was held out that the end must be near. The end of days was not a frightening event for the Jews of old. It was to be their greatest age, in which God himself judged all other nations as unworthy and rewarded those Jews who followed their God. Obedience to God was judged on how well one adhered to God's law and commandments.

The belief of divine recompense has echoed through history, changing the ways that both Christian and Jews have viewed their world and their destiny.

Even though the texts presented here are not in our western Christian canon, do not think they have not influenced our faith. The Dead Sea Scrolls provide insight into how Jews of the time thought, believed, and acted, but more than that, the texts were circulated and therefore bolstered and broadcast the doctrine and history they contained.

Documents, doctrine, and points of faith not found in our Bible tremendously influenced what has come to be the Judaism and Christianity we know and practice today.

TheWar Scroll

Index

General Meaning of Numbers in the Scriptures.

Number   Meaning

1 Unity. New beginnings, primacy – Hear o Israel, the Lord thy God is One.

2 Division, differences, opposition, Witnessing

3 Divine completeness, fullness

4 Creation, limits of the physical world; Creative works, elements, testing

5 Grace, favor, God's goodness; Holy Spirit, Pentateuch

6 Weakness and greatness of man. Man falling short of the Glory of God. Imperfection, family, tribe.

7 Perfection Resurrection; Spiritual completeness; Fathers perfection, Righteousness

8 Justice, Judgment, New birth; New beginnings, to abound, be strong, healthy.

9 Fruit of the spirit; Finalization. Conclusion, ending, completeness.

10 Divine order, Testimony; Law and responsibility, commandments. Newness

11   Disorder and judgment, cooperation lost to ego

12   Governmental perfection, Theocracy

13   Apostasy; depravity and rebellion, testing

14   Deliverance; Salvation, grace (see 5)

15   Rest, family (see 6)

16   Love, inner search

17   Dispensation, Victory, Judging

18   Bondage, ending (also see 9)

19   Faith, New starts

20   Redemption, confirming witness

21   Expectancy, waiting, torn completeness

22   Light, Disintegration, foundation of good

23   Death, release (see 5)
24   The Priesthood, service (see 6)
25   Repentance; The forgiveness of sins (see 7)
26   The Gospel of Christ
27   Preaching of the Gospel
28   Eternal life
29   Departure
30   Blood of Christ; Dedication (see 3)
31   Offspring, forming alliances
32   Covenant, grace (see 5)
33   Promise, minister (see 6)
34   Naming of a son (see 7)
35   Hope, Lawful judge (see 8)
36   Enemy, halting
37   The word of our Father
38   Slavery
39   Disease
40   Trials, Testing, chastisement, purification
42   Israel's oppression; First advent
44   Judgement of the World
45   Preservation
50   Holy Spirit; Pentecost (see 5)
60   Pride
66   Idol worship
70   To be made perfect, restoration of Israel; Universality
100   Election; Children of the promise
119   Spiritual perfection and victory 7*17=119
120   Divine period of probation
144   The Spirit guided life
200   Insufficiency
600   Warfare
666   Antichrist
777   Christ
888   Holy Spirit; The sum of Tree of Life

1000 Divine completeness and Fathers glory

4000 Salvation of the world through the blood of the
Lamb (Chose between Christ and Antichrist).

6000 Deception of Antichrist; Second advent

7000 Final judgment

144,000 Those numbered of Israel. The holy ones

The War Scroll

Joseph Lumpkin

Other fine books and ancient texts can be found at Fifth Estate Publishing or on the web at www.fifthestatepub.com

www.ingramcontent.com/pod-product-compliance
Lightning Source LLC
Chambersburg PA
CBHW072143270326
41931CB00010B/1872